The
Chameleon
Book of
LASTs

Never-to-be-repeated moments from a
world that is gone for ever

CHRISTOPHER SLEE

QUID EST VERITAS
EST VIR QUI ADEST

British Library Cataloguing in Publication Data
Slee, Christopher 1948-
The Chameleon book of lasts : (never-to-be-repeated
moments from a world that is gone for ever)
I. Title
032.02

ISBN 1-871469-31-7

Typeset in Palatino.
Input by the author using an Apple Macintosh™
computer and PageMaker® software.
Output by JMS Design St Ives Cambs.

Printed and bound in the United Kingdom by
Redwood Press Limited Melksham Wilts.

The Chameleon Book of LASTs

Christopher Slee was born in Africa in 1948. After completing his formal education in England he was commissioned into the Royal Engineers where he learned to combine his passions for both history and technology.

He was a parliamentary candidate for the Alliance in the 1983 British general election.

Married, with two children, Christopher Slee lives in Cambridgeshire and has interests in magazine publishing.

For my parents
Alan and Elaine

Contents

Illustrations

Illustration acknowledgements:
pages 105, 130 and 149 courtesy of the Illustrated London News Picture Library;
pages 30, 51, 55, 65, 75, 114, 141 and 165 courtesy of the Mary Evans Picture Library;
page 105 courtesy of Peter Newark's Military Pictures.

Foreword

More are men's ends mark'd than their lives before:
The setting sun, and music at the close,
As the last taste of sweets, is sweetest last,
Writ in remembrance more than things long past.

William Shakespeare

All beginnings eventually have endings – and endings have always fascinated me. Yet, whereas firsts tend by their nature to be announced and recorded for posterity, lasts seem often to slip into obscurity unchronicled.

I am an incorrigible collector of lasts. Those presented here are a personal selection drawn from 19th century Britain, a period marked by great social and technological change and thus a fertile period for the avid hunter of lasts. Some of these lasts were historically important with repercussions that affect us today. Others were simply trivial or outrageously bizarre. Yet every last makes a statement about the era that precedes it and is thus worthy of commemoration.

The opportunity to thank all those who assisted me in the research and writing of this book must not be missed. These were the staff in various of the Cambridgeshire libraries, particularly at Huntingdon; also at the Public Record Office, Kew, the National Maritime Museum, Greenwich, and the Central Reference Library, Westminster.

Thanks too must go to Andrew Fenton for some essential early direction and to Stephen Essberger for many different forms of encouragement on the scope and theme of this, the world's very first book of lasts.

Holywell   Christopher Slee
Cambridgeshire   1990

1 The LAST of the Irish Parliament

1 January 1801

Westminster, the 'Mother of Parliaments', reigned supreme in Great Britain and without real challenge throughout the 19th century. This was not always the case. Before and since other legislative bodies have had responsibilities over some of the peoples of the British Isles. Both Scotland and Ireland had independent sovereign Parliaments, under the same crown as England, at certain times in the past. Scotland's independent Parliament disappeared in 1707, to be subsumed in the English Parliament at Westminster. Ireland's Parliament lasted until the first day of the century, 1 January 1801.

When Britain was at war with France, in the last years of the 18th century, Ireland was, as usual, experiencing considerable unrest. Catholics were strongly discriminated against, having no right to vote, to be elected to office or to occupy the most important positions in public life. The Irish Parliament in Dublin was modelled on that at Westminster. It had an upper House of Lords and a lower House of Elected Members. Whilst nominally independent it could not pass legislation that was against the interests of mainland Britain. It was in any case strongly manipulated and controlled by the British Government through the powers of its mouthpiece in Ireland, the Lord Lieutenant installed in Dublin Castle.

Moves for radical political and religious reform were strong and growing stronger. One such movement led by a group called the 'United Irishmen', was inevitably exploited and supported by the French. An insurrection in 1798 was put down by the British military with the usual ruthlessness.

The British Government decided that it had had enough. After much debate it was decided to unify the Irish Parliament with that of Great Britain. In 1800 the Act of Union was passed, in both houses of both Parliaments. This act abolished the separate Irish Parliament in Dublin and, in effect, created the United Kingdom of Great Britain and Ireland.

The Irish were given a hundred seats in the Westminster Parliament. In addition, in Westminster's House of Lords, they were granted places for twenty-eight Irish peers, elected for life from among their own number by fellow Irish lords, and four Irish bishops from the now unified Anglican Church of England and Ireland.

A major part of the process of persuading the Irish to relinquish their own Parliament had been the open bribes paid to the patrons of the Irish 'pocket boroughs'. They made up the major part of the old Irish House of Commons. These constituencies, without a broad franchise or a secret ballot, were totally in the control of the owners of the land. To compensate the landowners for their loss of influence and power they were paid £15,000 per seat. A total sum of £1.25 million was paid out by the British Government. The Marquis of Downshire, ironically a vigorous opponent of the Act, was reputedly the most generously compensated for his many pocket seats.

The last sitting of the old Irish Parliament was on 2 August 1800, the day after the Act of Union received the royal assent. A 500 year old institution was dead. Dublin remained the centre of governmental administration for Ireland but its political heart had been torn out. The splendid Parliament buildings were sold to the Bank of Ireland. A stipulation was that the interior be altered so that all trace of its previous use be obliterated. Despite this, the House of Lords, 'the Old House in College Green', remains today much as it was in its 18th century glory.

As a result of the Act Ireland became part of the United Kingdom on 1 January 1801. Westminster would provide direct rule for over a hundred years until 1922 when the Irish Free State formed its own Parliament, the Dáil, but alas, not in the old buildings.

–

The Act did not solve the religious problems of Ireland at all. Although it gave Catholics the vote, it did not give them the right to become members of Parliament. The ascendancy of the Protestant minority over the Catholic majority was maintained for many more years.

As for the political problems, agitation for Irish Home Rule started almost immediately; it has never been far from the surface of the boiling pot of Irish politics, north and south, ever since.

2 Nelson's LAST words

21 October 1805

Much is on record of Admiral Lord Nelson's end. How he commanded the British fleet at Trafalgar and vanquished the combined French and Spanish fleets under Villeneuve is so well documented as to defy repetition. How he refused to cover his medals and stars on his uniform, even if it did make him a more obvious target to the enemy, was typical of the man. 'In honour I gained them, and in honour I will die with them,' he is reported to have said when urged to make himself less conspicuous during the fighting.

At the height of the battle, pacing the quarterdeck of his flagship *Victory*, he was eventually hit by one of the many sharpshooters positioned in the mizzen top of the French ship *Redoutable* alongside. The musket ball penetrated his left shoulder from above, entered his lung and broke his spine. He fell to the deck exclaiming 'They have done for me at last.' The captain of the *Victory*, Hardy, his ever faithful friend, was with him at the time.

He was carried below, his decorations and face covered with a handkerchief to avoid upsetting the ship's company at this critical moment in the battle.

Nelson was obviously dying, as the surgeon Dr Beatty soon discovered. The battle raged above him as he lay in the cockpit, the surgery of the huge wooden-walled ship. The superiority of the British ships and crews, combined with Nelson's strategy and leadership, left no doubt as to the outcome. The enemy ships were striking their colours, surrendering, with an inevitable regularity. Nelson demanded a visit from Hardy who eventually left the deck to visit his old friend.

Nelson was obsessed with 'duty'. This was apparent in the famous signal he sent to the fleet before the battle: 'England expects that every man will do his duty.' Along with his mistress, Lady Emma Hamilton, duty again occupied his mind during his last hours. At about four o'clock in the afternoon Hardy came down to see Nelson for the second and last time. He congratulated the admiral on the victory which was now nearly complete.

'Take care of my dear Lady Hamilton, Hardy: take care of poor

Lady Hamilton,' Nelson urged Hardy. And then, 'Kiss me Hardy.' His friend knelt down and kissed him on the cheek. 'Now I am satisfied. Thank God, I have done my duty.' Hardy returned to the deck.

Nelson now sank fast. His thirst increased, his pain became more and more severe and his voice grew faint. His thoughts were with his dear Emma and their daughter Horatia.

The ship's chaplain, Scott was at his side massaging his chest to bring some relief. Nelson repeated several times, 'I thank God I have done my duty.' His voice faded to to a whisper. His last words were 'God and my country' and then he died.

Nelson's verve and leadership had undoubtedly put an end to Napoleon's aspirations for the invasion of England. His body was returned to England and buried in St Paul's Cathedral after one of the most splendid state funerals London has ever seen. His brother inherited his title with a fantastically generous estate as a gift from the nation. His sisters received large grants of money but his mistress and daughter, ignored and forgotten by the nation, lived out the rest of their lives in poverty.

3 Pitt the Younger's LAST speech

9 November 1806

William Pitt, whom history calls 'Pitt the Younger' to distinguish him from his father of the same name, is usually remembered as the youngest ever British prime minister. The younger Pitt entered the House of Commons at the age of twenty-one. By the age of twenty-four he was Prime Minister. There can be fewer faster rises to power than his and it was the start of a brilliant political career during the crucial years between the American War of Independence and the wars with Napoleon's France. By the time Pitt was forty, he was prematurely aged and in poor health. He made his last speech on 9 November 1805 at Guildhall in London and died a few weeks later much mourned by the entire country.

Pitt was destined for a Parliamentary career at a very early age.

His father, William Pitt (known as 'the Elder'), who became the Earl of Chatham, was prime minister under George II and George III.

The younger Pitt went to Cambridge University at the age of fourteen and was member of Parliament for the pocket borough of Appleby when twenty-one. Remembering his father's performances in the House of Commons, great things were expected of him. With breathtaking confidence he immediately declared that he would only be accepting the very highest cabinet posts.

Edmund Burke, deeply moved after listening to his maiden speech, declared that he wasn't just a chip off the old block 'but the old block itself!'

His confidence was immense. At the age of twenty-three, after turning down lesser posts he became chancellor of the exchequer under Lord Shelburne. This ministry was soon voted out of office. Pitt was then offered the job of prime minister by the King but he refused knowing that he did not yet have enough parliamentary support. In the autumn of 1783 he was once again asked to form a government. This time he accepted and at the age of twenty-four became Britain's youngest ever prime minister.

He governed Britain continuously for seventeen years. During these years Pitt rebuilt the economy after the debilitating War of American Independence. He consolidated the years of peace by encouraging trade and commerce, he made Britain great by his statesmanship. These years, until 1792 when the wars with France broke out, were his most successful.

In 1801, after an argument with the King over Catholic emancipation, Pitt resigned from office. The war with France was brought to an end but by May 1803 it was renewed with more vigour than ever.

In May 1804, after three years out of office, Pitt was once again asked to form a ministry and he brought together members of all parties to prosecute the war.

Pitt's health was fading. His resort to the bottle under the enormous pressure of responsibility did not help his health or his appearance. He had considerable money problems. He had remained unmarried and eventually relied heavily on his niece to help him control his personal finances and run his household.

For Britain, Napoleon's victory at Ulm was only partly alleviated by the mixture of sad and glad tidings of Nelson's death and victory at Trafalgar. The day after this news reached England, Pitt rode to Guildhall to make what was to be his last speech. He was given a hero's welcome and toasted as the 'Saviour of Europe'.

With characteristic modesty Pitt declined the accolade and replied with one of his shortest speeches, 'I return your many thanks for the honour you have done me, but Europe is not to be saved by any single man. England has saved herself by her exertions, and will, as I trust, save Europe by her example.'

Pitt was exhausted. Suffering from gout and cirrhosis of the liver, he went to Bath to convalesce. There news reached him of another crushing victory for Napoleon at Austerlitz. Pitt was shattered when he returned to London in the new year, to his house in Putney. He never recovered and two weeks later, in the early hours of 23 January, he died muttering the words, 'O my country, how I love my country.'

—

Pitt's reputation as the 'pilot that weathered the storm' survives to this day. For a great many years he held a position – and the power that went with it – that is unique in British history. His political integrity was seldom in question; in his private life he was without scandal. The ending of his career in full flight, at an early age when his country needed him most, was a shattering blow to war-weary Britain at the height of the Napoleonic wars.

4 The LAST of the House of Stuart

13 July 1807

The first sovereign of both England and Scotland, Britain's first member of the House of Stuart, was King James the First of England and the Sixth of Scotland. The troubled and autocratic dynasty that succeeded him lasted just over a hundred years on the throne and a further hundred in exile. His son Charles I was beheaded by the Parliamentarians after the Civil War; his grandson James II was chased off the throne over the issue of Roman Catholicism. His great-grand-daughter Anne was the last Stuart sovereign to sit on the British throne. That was not,

however, the last of the dynasty. Henry Stuart, Cardinal, Duke of York was the last legitimate male Stuart claimant to the British throne.

The birth in 1688 of James II's son, by his second marriage to the Roman Catholic Mary of Modena, was one of the issues which precipitated the 'Glorious Revolution'. The British ruling classes would not accept the prospect of little James Edward growing up to rule over them, yet another Catholic and despotic king. Instead they invited the Prince of Orange and his wife (James II's daughter) Mary to rule over them as joint sovereigns – William III and Mary II.

Two major 18th century rebellions were the result of this dynastic split. In Scotland in 1715 James Edward, then styled James III, tried to claim his crown. He failed. In 1745 his son, the 'Young Pretender' known as Bonnie Prince Charlie, tried again on his father's behalf. His invasion of England came close to success but he was forced to retreat and his army was finally defeated at Culloden. The Stuarts retired to the continent where, in the Roman Catholic courts, with varying degrees of social success, they lived out the rest of their days in peace.

Bonnie Prince Charlie married in later life but had no children and died in 1788. His younger brother Henry survived him and 'reigned' over the now dwindling band of Stuart adherents, acclaimed as 'King Henry IX'.

On his birth Henry had been unofficially created Duke of York by his father. He grew up to be a mild-mannered Prince who took to his religion with great fervour. His attempts to help his brother in the '45 rebellion came to nothing; the troops he raised failed to reach Scotland. He was made a cardinal deacon by Pope Benedict XIV in 1747 and took priestly orders the following year. Various bishoprics and archbishoprics followed in a routinely successful career within the upper ranks of the Catholic Church in Europe.

–

Henry proved to be no threat to the ruling Hanoverians back in Britain. Near the end of his life, after he lost all his possessions in Italy to Napoleon's army, George III even granted him a suitable annual pension. The 'Cardinal King' was a pious man. He never set foot in Britain and ended his days quietly in Frascati on 13 July 1807. He was buried in St Peter's, Rome.

5 The LAST slave trading

25 March 1807

**The slave trade was one of the international commercial activities
that made Britain one of the major world powers of the 18th
century. It had been started, almost casually, by Elizabethan
adventurers and explorers but culminated in a well organised
export business, earning huge profits, run primarily from the
ports of Liverpool, London and Bristol. Trading in slaves for all
British companies was finally abolished by law in 1807.**

For British business the slave trade was a means whereby the
products of British industry could be sold abroad. English cloth
particularly and other goods were shipped to the west coast of
Africa. Here they were exchanged for slaves. The slave cargoes
were then carried across the Atlantic ocean, under conditions of
great cruelty (the infamous 'middle passage') to be sold in the
West Indies and America. The ships returned to their English ports
laden with sugar, tobacco and, of course, cotton to be manufactured
into more cloth for later export.

The perpetrators of this barbarous trade were uniquely shielded
from the sights of their cruelty. The prosperous merchants and
their families in Liverpool and Bristol avoided all real contact with
this trading in human misery. All they saw were trading goods
leaving port in their ships, exotic products returning from the
West Indies – and money accumulating in their banks.

About 200 ships, 'slavers', were involved in the trade, carrying
annually about 50,000 slaves from Africa.

The first serious attempt by the British Government to stop the
trade was in 1806 when a law was passed which forbade the re-
export of slaves from British colonies. This stopped slaves sold in
the West Indies being sold on to plantations in the USA. William
Wilberforce was one the men behind this law. The primary export
of slaves from Africa, however, continued.

For the future, Charles Fox pledged in the House of Commons
that 'The African slave trade was contrary to the principles of
justice and humanity and would, with all practicable expedition,
be abolished.'

A year later the Government led by Lord Grenville found itself with two pledges to carry out: Catholic emancipation and the abolition of the slave trade, both in the teeth of opposition from the King and many of the aristocracy. It pushed Catholic emancipation to one side and chose to address the slavery issue.

In the House of Lords a rearguard action, fought by many of the lords with the assistance of a few slave captains called to give evidence, proved too weak. The measure to abolish the trade was passed in both houses and became law on 25 March 1807.

The slave merchants were still given a few months' grace. They had until May to depart from the country on the their last trip; the year's end to cease their trade. The last few months were cruelly hectic for British slavers and the slaves crammed even more tightly into the dark holds. But by 1 January 1808 the last legal cargo of human beings had been landed in the West Indies.

At the Congress of Vienna in 1814 Britain persuaded most other European nations to impose similar bans on their slave traders.

–

Slavery of course continued, even in British colonies. Total emancipation and freedom for slaves was to take many more years yet. Illegal slave trading by British captains and trading by other nations also continued. They too were to take many more years to disappear.

6 The LAST of the ducking stool
1809

A curious method of punishment, mainly for women, was in use in Britain from the 17th century – the ducking stool and ducking pond. It was used for the fairly trivial offences of 'quarreling' and 'gossiping' but sometimes for blatant dishonesty – excessive watering down of beer was a common example. It seldom, however, resulted in lasting damage to the victim. She was tied to a stool or chair which was attached to the end of a long beam. The beam was positioned, see-saw fashion, close to edge of a pond. Controlled from the bank by a village official and some stout lads the offender would be dipped into the water. The use of ducking stools (sometimes called 'cucking' stools) ceased completely in the early 19th century.

The last recorded instance of someone being 'officially' ducked in a ducking pond was in 1809 at Leominster when Jenny Pipes was the offender. Eight years later officials of that same town – obviously fanatical supporters of this particular method of punishment – were unable to carry out a similar sentence on Sarah Leeke as the ducking pond was found to be completely dry.

Many towns and villages had ducking ponds and the associated apparatus of ducking stool. It was an alternative to stocks and, although the justice was rough, it was cheap and quick and even provided some enjoyment to the public.

Today, at the site of Westminster's own ducking pond, exuberant revellers still take soakings, usually voluntarily, in London's Trafalgar Square fountains.

7 The LAST of the Tower Mint

1810

Coins of the realm were first made at a London mint in the year AD825. When the Normans built the Tower of London, the Tower Mint was charged with manufacturing much of England's coinage and medals. In about 1300 this was established on a formal footing and lasted until 1810, when the Mint outgrew its premises at the Tower and was moved to buildings nearby.

The main part of the Royal Mint at the Tower was a huge room, between the inner and outer walls, in which many workers were employed in a foundry and rolling mills, turning out the sovereign's coinage. Bars of gold and silver were melted down to produce the coins that were to lubricate Britain's financial machine for over five centuries. The Royal Mint had overall control of the design of the coinage and, for much of its time at the Tower, produced all of the coinage.

But it was not only the manufacture of coins that established the Royal Mint as an important financial institution. Before banks were commonplace, the merchants of London would store their money at the Tower Mint – that is, until the Civil War when Charles I appropriated all the spare cash there to help with his war effort. Thereafter the commercial firms in London decided that London's goldsmiths were more trustworthy as the guardians of their money – and they paid interest too.

For much of its time at the Tower the Royal Mint employed some of the finest jewellery craftsmen and engravers in the country. Charles II, when he returned from his French exile, brought with him John Rotier, a Frenchman who became responsible for some of the best coinage ever produced at the Tower. The dramatic improvements in the portraiture can be seen on the coinage of that time. His famous design for 'Britannia', still seen on today's coins, was based on one of the King's mistresses, the beautiful Frances Stuart, Duchess of Richmond.

The office of master of the mint was an honorary position, once held with some distinction by Sir Isaac Newton. The post was abolished in 1870, the position now being nominally held by the chancellor of the exchequer.

The Royal Mint, along with the menagerie and the armoury were firm 'tourist' attractions by the end of the 18th century. Thousands of Londoners were greatly intrigued by the Mint and its vast display of visible wealth.

But times were changing: the Tower was not a suitable place for a modern factory and the pressure of space made the move inevitable. Premises were found at nearby Little Tower Hill and the end of the Royal Mint at the Tower of London came in 1810.

–

In 1968, the Tower Hill premises too were found unsuitable and the Royal Mint was moved to Llantrisant in Wales. Since 1975 no coins have been minted at all at Tower Hill and in 1980 the shop and exhibition centre were closed for redevelopment.

8 The LAST execution of escaped convicts

1810

A sentence of 'transportation for life' meant what it said at the beginning of the 19th century. It was a capital offence for a convict who managed to escape from one of the penal colonies and return to Britain. Those few who made it back to the home country and were eventually caught by the authorities were hanged. The last illegally returned convict was hanged in 1810 although this penalty was only officially abolished in 1834.

Transportation as a punishment remained in full swing in the 1830s. The same year that capital punishment for this offence was officially abolished, the Tolpuddle Martyrs were sentenced to transportation for seven years after being convicted of forming an illegal trade union.

Charles Dickens in his book *Great Expectations* gives Magwitch, the illegally returned convict, a literal fear of death on being caught – but with true artistic licence Dickens was exaggerating since the law had already been changed.

–

Despite the abolition of capital punishment for unlawfully returning from transportation, the distance from Australia made it very difficult to return, even for those who had their full 'ticket-of-leave' to do so. Most freed convicts settled in the Antipodes and formed an important element of the make-up of the Australian nation.

9 The LAST regency

1811 - 1820

Several times in British history a regent has been appointed to act on behalf of and to carry out the duties of the sovereign. The appointment of a regent is required, under established law, when the monarch is incapacitated, otherwise unavailable or under eighteen years of age at the time of succession. The last instance of a regency in Britain was in 1811 when the Prince of Wales, the future George IV, was appointed, his father George III having been declared insane.

Custom demands that to recognise a need for a regent at least three people, from among a list of specified high office holders, must declare the monarch to be incapacitated. It is also now accepted that the next in line to the throne, if over eighteen years old, should if possible be appointed the regent. Otherwise it would be expected to be another close relative.

This has not always been so. Regents in the past have often been ruthless outsiders, using their real power behind the throne to amass great fortunes and to appoint their own men to important offices.

George III had exhibited signs of insanity for many years before 1811. When a previous serious bout of madness was causing concern in 1788 a Regency Bill, introduced to Parliament by Pitt, was halted by the immediate and very opportune recovery of the King. By 1810 however the King's insanity was too far gone. The Prince of Wales too was champing at the bit and Parliament had no alternative but to act. After the due process of Parliamentary business he was sworn in as Prince Regent on 6 February 1811. His powers at first were slightly restricted, in the creation of peers and appointment of salaries, but these were lifted a year later. This appointment heralded a period of high spending and lavish living for 'Prinny'. When his father died in 1820 he continued his dissolute lifestyle as King.

The 'Regency' period, 1811-20, is now regarded as a time of high culture and 'society', with much interest in the arts and architecture.

−

A more recent regency nearly took place. Queen Victoria succeeded to the throne on 20 June 1837 at the age of 18 years and one month. Had her uncle, William IV, died just a few weeks earlier it is probable that her mother, the Duchess of Kent, would have been regent until Victoria had reached her eighteenth birthday.

10 The LAST guinea

1813

The golden guinea is a coin which conjures up images of treasure and adventure, gambling and lavish spending. In fact it was the major high value coin in the currency of the British realm for the latter part of the 18th century. Its general issue as a coin had ceased by the start of the 19th century but a special minting was made in 1813 to pay the Army which was fighting in the Peninsular War. This was the last issue of the guinea coin.

The guinea had several different values in its long lifetime. It was first introduced in 1663 and valued at 20s (£1). The gold from which it was made originally came from Guinea in West Africa and so the coin was nicknamed the 'guinea'. The first coins even had a small elephant emblem on the obverse below King Charles I's bust, to commemorate the origin of the metal.

At the beginning of William and Mary's reign the guinea was officially valued at 21s 6d. In subsequent years it often reached as much as 30s due to the generally poor state of the other (silver) coinage.

By the time of the Napoleonic wars the value of the guinea had been re-established at 21s. Due to the shortage of bullion, however, guineas were last issued for general public circulation in 1799. Bank notes and other token money were first issued at this time on a large scale.

In 1813 the very last guinea was minted. On the obverse the bust of George III was by Marchant and the reverse displayed the royal coat-of-arms surrounded by the garter. It was exclusively used to pay the British army then engaged in fighting in Spain and Portugal. At the same time a half-guinea coin of similar design was also issued. There was even a third-guinea coin. Due to the extreme shortage of silver the third-guinea coin (value 7s) helped to fill the gap.

After the war, the Gold Standard was adopted and a complete 'recoinage' began. The guinea was replaced by the gold 20s sovereign.

—

Long after the coin's disappearance, the guinea continues to be used as a unit of currency, mainly in charging for some of the traditional professional services, in the 'classier' shops and in many auction sales.

The guinea of 1813 has since become known as the 'Military' guinea. It is very rare and is highly sought after by collectors.

11 The LAST of the 'fir' frigates

November 1814

Most of the 'wooden walls', the magnificent square-rigged ships of the line of the Royal Navy, were constructed of oak, one of the hardest woods available in the northern hemisphere. A first rate ship, carrying a 100 guns or more, required over a quarter of a million cubic feet of solid timber, obtained from some seventy-five acres of mature oak forest.

During the Napoleonic wars, as the Royal Navy maintained and expanded its influence around the world, more and more ships were needed. In a desperate measure to make up for the shortage of oak, some fifty of the smaller ships of the line, fourth and fifth rate frigates, were made of imported softwoods, mainly from Canada. These ships had a relatively short life but were cheaper and quicker to build. They plugged a vital gap in the Navy's ship-building programme and became known as the 'fir' frigates, serving with distinction alongside their tougher-hulled sisters. The last of these fir frigates, was the *Leander*, commissioned in 1814. She was finally broken up in 1830.

When Britain became locked in war with France at the end of the 18th century the Royal Navy soon realised that their normal ship-building programme would have to be accelerated. Hard woods were becoming scarce and for the smaller ships softwoods were a viable option. Earlier that century some softwood ships had been built but were regarded as failures as they had such a short life in the water.

The toredo worm was the enemy of all ships' hulls. It attacked the wooden planking, burrowing deep into the timber causing major structural problems. As a measure of protection all hulls were covered in copper sheathing. If this was well fastened and

27

regularly maintained it gave the hardwood hulls many years of service; some ships lasted over a hundred years. The softwoods were not so easily protected. Fixing the copper sheets in place with copper nails was difficult; they worked loose and the ships had to pay regular visits to dockyards to be re-sheathed. In addition the softwoods were especially susceptible to rot. However, in times when ships were expected to take heavy gunfire directly into their hulls from close quarters, the question of whether a hull could last ten, fifteen or even a hundred years was regarded as somewhat academic.

Various softwoods were tried: pitch pine, red pine and yellow pine; all generally (and incorrectly) called 'fir'.

In 1812, just as the war at sea was all but won and the ship shortage seemingly solved, Britain managed to embroil herself in another war, this time with America. Frigates were needed on the USA's eastern seaboard and the construction of what was to be the last batch of softwood frigates was begun.

The *Leander* was one of the last of these ships to be constructed. The keel was laid in June 1813 at Wigram and Green's shipyard on the river Thames at Blackwall. She was constructed in pitch pine and was launched a few months later in November. From Blackwall she was towed round to dry-dock at Greenwich where the copper sheathing was nailed in place.

Leander carried fifty-eight guns, twenty-six of the 42-pounder carronades and thirty-two of the long 24-pounders. She had a tonnage of 1,572, was 174 feet long at the water line and had a beam of 45 feet. In February 1814 she sailed with a full crew for the USA, Captain Sir George Ralph Collier in command.

By June she was already in action, capturing a 16-gun American ship, the *Rattlesnake*. Later the *Leander* was involved in a famous action, along with two other Royal Navy ships (both also fir frigates), against the USA's *Constitution* off the Cape Verde Islands. In the very short time before the war was over the *Leander* gained a respectable reputation with the Americans and considerable glory for the Royal Navy.

In 1815, when the wars with both France and the USA were over, the *Leander* already needed repairs to her hull. In 1816 the ship took part in the bombardment of Algiers, was in the midst of the action and suffered heavy casualties.

Leander was completely re-coppered twice more in the next

three years and in 1822 was docked at Portsmouth and taken out of active service. Here she rotted away for several years until in March 1830 she was put out of her misery and 'taken to pieces', finally broken up, the very last surviving fir frigate of the Royal Navy.

It is appropriate that the 'Leander' name lived on. The habit which the Royal Navy has of using its famous ships' names over and over again, means that the present-day Leander class frigates have their roots, in name at least, in an inauspicious class of softwood sailing ships constructed in a great hurry at the the beginning of the 19th century.

12 The LAST Thames frost fair

February 1814

One of the more reliable sources of information on past weather patterns has been the recorded occasions when major rivers have frozen over. Before proper scientific meteorological records were kept, from about the middle of the 19th century, detailed analysis on what the weather was like in the past is difficult. One of the firmest indications of exceptionally cold winters has been the dates when London's river Thames has been frozen over.

The freezing of the Thames was certainly quite regular throughout most of the 17th and 18th centuries, occurring perhaps a couple of times in a generation, perhaps as much as once every decade. It was still obviously an exceptionally notable event and when it occurred large markets, fairs and entertainment of all kinds were held on the ice. These sometimes went on for many days and weeks. The festivities were known as 'frost fairs' and the last occasion when the Thames was frozen hard enough for this to happen was in the winter of 1813-14. Sheep were roasted in the middle of the river and skittles and other games were played with great gusto.

Early in 1814 an elephant was actually led onto the ice. To the amazement and astonishment of the thousands of assembled

Revelries on the Thames ice during
the winter of 1813-14, the last
occasion when a Thames Frost Fair
was held. The rebuilding of London
Bridge in the 1830s allowed the river
to flow much faster and ice has never
formed right across the river since.

Londoners, the animal made a crossing of the Thames downstream of Blackfriars Bridge. This is certainly the first and last recorded instance.

On 6 February 1814, the ice gave way and the Thames had seen its last frost fair.

–

The early years of the 19th century proved to be the last years of what is now referred to as a 'mini' ice age. The river Thames has however been frozen since – in February 1895 it was cold enough for the ice upstream of the City to support skating for several weeks. Unfortunately the ice was too lumpy and not strong enough for a regular fair to be held.

13 Britain's LAST battle with the USA

9 January 1815

In 1812 the United States of America declared war on the United Kingdom. Two and a half years later the war was brought to an inconclusive end; the last fighting in that war, which proved to be the last armed conflict between the two countries, was the Battle of New Orleans in January 1815. The British troops led by the ill-fated Sir Edward Pakenham, who died in the battle, were defeated by the Americans led by Andrew Jackson, a future US president.

The war was essentially over the USA's right to neutrality. There were also other more emotive issues, such as American sailors being press-ganged into service with the Royal Navy. American trade with Europe was blockaded and constantly interfered with by the British. Napoleon, who was keen to foment hostilities between the two countries to help his own cause, was also involved. In the end, the war was too late to help the French and, just as the British Government were about to lift the blockade, the USA lost patience and declared war.

Most of the fighting took place on the Canadian border. The USA, greatly outnumbering British and Canadian colonial forces made some headway. But, considering their numbers and short lines of communications, they made little long-term progress.

31

The incident when British troops captured Washington and burned the presidential mansion is famous because on rebuilding it the Americans painted it white, to hide the scars of violence. Ever since it has been called the White House.

At sea the Royal Navy understandably had the best of it.

At the end of 1814, it was decided to move a British contingent to the south, to attack the Americans at the mouth of the Mississippi river.

General Pakenham landed his troops and supplies, complete with heavy cannon, and they made their way up the river bank towards New Orleans. Hostilities began in December at Bonaventura with the British opening up with their surprisingly well-placed guns. The Americans after much initial confusion managed to bring their own artillery into action and drive off the attackers forcing them to abandon their guns. A new plan was devised by Pakenham which involved capturing the Americans' guns to turn them on themselves. Cutting a section of canal to bring in new supplies also figured prominently in the preparations. The final assault from the British battalions came in the new year on 8 January. Pakenham's men, now reinforced and about 8,000 strong, were however soon thrown into confusion. The defences prepared by Jackson were almost unassailable and the redcoats had very little chance of success. Assault equipment was found to be missing and the attack on the enemy artillery was so long delayed as to be useless.

The American sharpshooters, firing from cover, picked off the officers one by one. Pakenham himself was killed along with 290 others; 1,262 were wounded and 484 were missing. The Americans suffered only a handful of casualties and the British limped back to their ships under the command of General Lambert. In moving his depleted forces along the coast and, in the last action of the war, capturing Fort Mobile in Alabama on 11 February, Lambert regained some of his pride if not the initiative.

By the time the Battle of New Orleans had been fought the war was in any case over. The news of the Treaty of Ghent concluding the hostilities was signed the previous year on 24 December. News travelled slowly, so an unnecessary battle in an even more unnecessary war was fought out ignominiously for the British forces in the swamps of Louisiana.

–

The battle, whilst it had no effect on the outcome of the war, did confirm the Americans' right to that part of their continent. In addition to establishing Jackson's reputation, the battle swept away any international doubts on the ownership of the Mississippi delta area and led to full scale Americanisation of the South West. In Britain the defeat was soon forgotten in the outpouring of sentiment over the Battle of Waterloo which finally defeated Napoleon later that year.

14 The LAST of the Luddites

1816

'Luddites' was the name given to groups of workers in the early part of the 19th century who protested violently against the introduction of new labour-saving machinery which was putting them out of work. The movement started in the textile industry in the Midlands in 1811. The last of the Luddite riots occurred in the Eastern Counties among agricultural workers in 1816.

When the workers in the cottage industries found their livelihoods threatened by new steam-driven machinery they tried to resist this by smashing the new machines and burning down the owners' homes. Several rioters and mill owners lost their lives and some highly organised pitched battles took place. Offenders were convicted, some were hanged and many more sentenced to transportation. Severe punishment quelled most of the ensuing violent confrontations in 1812.

The movement obtained its name from a series of semi-literate anonymous letters written to the press during the original riots in 1811 and 1812. The letters were always signed by 'Ned Ludd', 'General Ludd' or even 'King Ludd'. This name was a reference to a village idiot, Ned Ludd, in Leicestershire. Once when goaded beyond restraint he had burst into a cottage and broken some weaving machines. Ever afterwards, when machines were found broken, it was customary to say that 'Ned Ludd' had done it.

After the war with France was concluded the country was suffering under severe economic depression. Nowhere was this more apparent than amongst the farming community. Luddites sprung up again amongst farm labourers demanding higher wages and a fixed maximum price for bread. The last outburst of the so-called Luddite Movement occurred in 1816. Marching under a banner proclaiming 'Bread or Blood' the mob gathered at Littleport, in the heart of East Anglia. They smashed threshing machines and burned barns and houses. The local militia was called out to restore order and at least two of the Luddites were killed in the ensuing fighting. Over seventy of them were arrested.

At the trials following their arrests, thirty-four were condemned to be hanged but only five of the sentences were carried out. Some of the others were transported to Australia and many others were imprisoned for twelve month periods.

–

At the same time as the last of the Luddite riots, unrest elsewhere in the country was widespread, later developing into agitation for Parliamentary and other reforms. This radicalism was crushed with great severity by the Government.

The word 'Luddite' today is used to mean those who are opposed to industrial change; who would destroy new machinery rather than suffer the job losses often brought about by new inventions.

15 The LAST beheading

1 May 1820

One of the most gruesome forms of execution ever practised in Britain was that of 'hanging, drawing and quartering'. With this method – almost exclusively reserved for traitors – the offender was hanged until nearly dead, cut down, disembowelled and his entrails then burned in front of him. His body was then cut into four pieces and his head was cut off to be displayed on a nearby pike as a warning to others. The moment of death was difficult to establish but many victims survived to smell their own guts burning.

This devastatingly inhumane method of public execution had disappeared by the 19th century. However beheading was still left for traitors and this was last inflicted, in Britain, in 1820 when members of the Cato Street Conspiracy were beheaded for their part in trying to kill members of the Cabinet and overthrow the Government.

The years after 1815 were years of great unrest and distress for large parts of the population. Arthur Thistlewood was an active campaigner who had led the riots at Spa Fields in 1816. He had already spent a year in jail for libelling the Prince Regent and for issuing a challenge to a Government minister, Lord Sidmouth. He was a vigorous and colourful character and, by the standards of his day, a sincere advocate of reform.

In 1819 he devised plans to assassinate the key members of Lord Liverpool's Tory Cabinet. However, one of the members of his gang, Edwards, was a Government agent. Acting as an *agent provocateur* he had actively encouraged Thistlewood and the authorities thus knew all about the conspiracy from its beginnings.

Thistlewood and his fellows had learnt that members of the Cabinet were due to meet at a dinner in Grosvenor Square in February 1820. This was decided as the most convenient moment to strike. They were to rush in and slay all those present. Then, with the assistance of the mob which they expected to rise in their favour, they were to storm the Tower and the Bank of England and set up a provisional government of their own. It was a particularly harebrained scheme and, even had the authorities not known the details from the start, it had little chance of success.

The Cabinet however was fully informed since the conspirators had been deceived. At their final rendezvous at a house in Cato Street they were interrupted by the Bow Street Runners. In the ensuing struggle nine of the gang were arrested. Thistlewood killed one of the Runners by stabbing him in the chest and, with thirteen others, made his escape. He was arrested the next day at a friend's house in Moorfields, betrayed by the agent Edwards. Three of the gang were sentenced to transportation but the five ringleaders, including Thistlewood, were sentenced to die traitors' deaths.

On 1 May 1820, outside Newgate Prison, the usual place for executions in London, the five conspirators were hanged and then cut down to be beheaded by a masked executioner. For some reason the axe specially prepared for the purpose was not employed. Instead, a large surgeon's knife was used to hack off the heads before they were held aloft to the cry of 'Behold a Traitor!'

35

and the customary roars of approval from the thousands of spectators.

—

This was the last occasion of official beheadings in Britain. Thereafter even traitors were allowed to be buried in one piece. Hangings continued in Britain, in public and then behind closed doors, until 1963.

16 The LAST royal trial

10 November 1820

For many centuries British history was regularly punctuated with the trials of members of the royalty. They were accused, tried and convicted of serious charges. Female members were particularly vulnerable: King Henry VIII's wives, Anne Boleyn and Catherine Howard, although perhaps the best known, were not the only queens to have affairs that proved fatal. Most of these trials were riddled with hypocrisy; many had elements of farce. None had both these in such full measure as the last occasion of such royal trials in 1820, that of Queen Caroline, George IV's wife.

In 1795, when the Prince of Wales eventually succumbed to his father's pleadings to marry and produce an heir, he had already been secretly (and illegally) married for ten years to a quiet, devoted Catholic widow, Maria Fitzherbert.

A bigamous marriage to the brash and graceless Princess Caroline of Brunswick went ahead. Nine months later their heir, Princess Charlotte, was born. Duty done, 'Prinny' took his leave, never to return to the marriage bed.

Princess Caroline, a woman who was as unsuited to chastity and a quiet life as 'Prinny' himself, was soon involved in a series of public scandals with a number of men, many in public life, who visited her court at Blackheath on the outskirts of London. Her husband was predictably furious, despite his own continued affairs with a number of mistresses and reconciliation with his 'other' wife Maria. In 1811, when the Prince of Wales was made Regent, one of his first actions was to remove his daughter from her mother's keeping.

Caroline became increasingly ostracised from society and in 1814 she moved to the Continent where her behaviour became more and more vulgar and flagrant. She left a trail of ex-lovers all over Europe and became a social outcast. In Italy she became involved with a former cavalry quartermaster, Bartolomeo Bergami. She was ignored by society to such an extent that she only learned by accident of her daughter's death in childbirth – she had not even been aware that she had married.

Early in 1820 the old, mad King of England died, the Regency was over and Caroline's husband became King George IV. She was 52 years old and, at last, the Queen of Great Britain and Ireland. She was determined to have her revenge on the society that had treated her so cruelly and at once set out to return to England. She arrived at Dover and such was the unpopularity of both the King and his Government that she was immediately taken up by the crowds and mobs in all the towns and cities on her way to London. Very soon she became the rallying point for all opposition. There were riots in the capital and troops had to be called out to keep order.

Within a month the Government had been peruaded to act; they knew that Caroline would have to be legally deprived of her position. They postponed the coronation and presented in the House of Lords a 'Bill of Pains and Penalties' 'to deprive Her Majesty Caroline Amelia Elizabeth of the Title, Prorogations, Rights, Priveleges and Pretensions of Queen Consort of this realm on the grounds of a most degrading intimacy between the Queen when Princess of Wales and Bartolomeo Bergami, a foreigner of low station.'

The gloves were off and the stakes, if not the very highest (death for treason, royal infidelity against the King, was not an option), were at least the most serious that a member of the royalty, the Queen no less, had faced for many years.

The Government's attempt to pass this Bill through both Houses of Parliament now became *de facto* the public trial of the Queen for adultery. The Parliament buildings were surrounded by heavy barricades to keep the mobs at bay, cavalry were stationed in the nearby streets and the river Thames was patrolled by armed boats.

At the start of the trial, to applause from the throng outside, the

37

Queen herself arrived at the Houses of Parliament in her new state landau drawn by six chestnut horses. Veiled and dressed in deep mourning, she swept into the House and, much to the Government's consternation, took her rightful place as a Peeress of the Realm to watch the proceedings.

Not all the noble lords supported the Bill; many were appalled at the entire proceedings. The fact that such a notorious *roué* as the King should have instigated such a harassment of his Queen was unacceptable to many of the more reputable politicians and public figures of the day. Despite strong pressures to attend and support the Bill they stayed away in protest.

The evidence was presented over several days; the Attorney-General put the case for the Government. Defending, for the Queen, was her personal attorney Lord Brougham. Witnesses were called; there was no lack of circumstantial evidence of the Queen's affair with Bergami. Servants, cooks and spies all were called to give their stories and be cross-examined. As the weeks passed the country was agog with the details; there was a serious possibility of civil war as the riots and disturbances from the Queen's supporters continued.

The House was convinced that the Queen was guilty yet the Lords knew that the King himself was even more so. Even if the Bill were passed and presented to the House of Commons they would undoubtedly throw it out anyway – and then there were the rioting mobs outside.

On a vote, the House of Lords did pass the Bill by a slender majority, finding against the Queen. But the Prime Minister, Lord Liverpool, a realist, had the Bill withdrawn on 10 November.

The jubilant mobs took part in celebrating the Queen's 'acquittal' in cities as far apart as Edinburgh, Dublin and Manchester, as well as in London itself for three nights in succession. The King was apoplectic with fury but the constitutional crisis passed.

Poor Queen Caroline was, however, done for. Officially humiliated and ignored despite being the legitimate Queen, she never recovered. The following year when trying to attend her husband's coronation she was forcibly turned away from the doors of Westminster Abbey to the derision of the watching crowds. She died at Hammersmith three weeks later, reviled and largely unloved, one of Britain's unhappier queens. Perversely, the ever capricious mob honoured her by rioting at her funeral.

The irony of Queen Caroline's acquittal – everyone in Parliament knew her to be guilty as charged – was matched only by the sheer hypocrisy of King George himself in pressing for the trial. His example of 'royal' behaviour too, it is thought, was the last of its kind.

17 The LAST king's champion
19 July 1821

The kings and queens of Britain have, over the years, exercised a right to nominate a champion to act on on their behalf in cases of a challenge to combat. Obviously the sovereign could not engage in combat personally, so the champion was appointed to carry out this task on his or her behalf. There is no record of a champion having to perform anything other than a ceremonial duty.

The King's champion seems to be unique to England and the idea originates in the feudal laws of the 14th century. His main duty came during the banquet held directly after the coronation – he rode on horseback into the assembled company to defend 'by his body, if necessary' anyone who dared challenge the new sovereign. The last occasion when this was performed was after the outrageously extravagant and lavish coronation of King George IV in 1821. Henry Dymoke was the champion.

The feast was held in Westminster Hall, a stone's throw from Westminster Abbey where the coronation had taken place. A series of wooden galleries had been constructed in the hall for spectators to watch the celebrations. After the first course had been served the champion was called in to do his duty. A flourish of trumpets heralded his arrival on a piebald charger, flanked by the Duke of Wellington as Lord High Constable and Lord Howard as Deputy Earl Marshall.

Dymoke read out his challenge at the gates to the hall:
'If any person of what degree soever, high or low, shall deny or gainsay our sovereign lord King George IV, of the United Kingdom of Great Britain and Ireland, defender of

the faith, son and next heir of our sovereign lord King George III, the last king deceased, to be right heir to the imperial crown of this United Kingdom, or that he ought not to enjoy the same, here is his champion, who saith that he lieth, and he is a false traitor; being ready in person to combat with him, and in this quarrel will adventure his life against him, on what day soever shall be appointed.'

He flung his gauntlet onto the stone floor. There was no-one to accept his challenge and it was returned to him by his esquire.

The party rode to the middle of the hall and the challenge was repeated. It was finally issued for the third and last time, amidst great applause from the assembled throng, at the steps leading to the royal banqueting table. His Majesty, now presumably relieved that there were no takers for the challenges, drank the health of his champion. He then passed the golden goblet to his champion who drank to His Majesty's health in turn with the cry, 'Long live his Majesty, King George IV!' The cup was passed to his page who bore it away for Dymoke family posterity.

The King soon left the hall to return to the palace.

The feast rapidly descended from sublime pomp into embarrassing farce. The guests and serving attendants now approached the deserted royal tables. Cautiously at first but then with increasing boldness, souvenirs of gold cutlery, plates, vases and many other portable items disappeared into the pockets of the surrounding crowd. The Lord High Chamberlain managed to push his way through the the crowd and save the more important items.

Even at the time the expense of the coronation was extensively criticised. The king's robes for the occasion cost £25,000 and were worn for only a few hours. The total cost was a quarter of a million pounds. The King's popularity, never high, was soon as low as ever in the country. Nine years later his brother William IV spent only £50,000 on his coronation.

—

Never again was the king's champion required to perform these official duties. The position of champion however still exists. It is hereditary, tied to the lordship of the manor of Scrivelsby in Lincolnshire since 1377 and the present incumbent is the direct descendant of the last active champion, Henry Dymoke.

18 Byron's LAST verse

19 April 1824

Lord Byron was one of the most colourful and eccentric poets of the 19th century. He died in self-imposed exile in Greece in 1824. He was almost exclusively concerned at the time with helping the Greek nation in their fight for independence against the Turks. He had already achieved huge acclaim in his native Britain and was now adored by the Greeks for his commitment to their cause. The last sad, rather desperate poetry he wrote, shortly before he tragically died, still a young man, dealt with his feelings for his friend and servant, a young Greek boy Loukas Chalandritsanos:

> Thus much and more; and yet thou lov'st me not,
> And never will! Love dwells in our will.
> Nor can I blame thee, though it be my lot
> To strongly, wrongly vainly love thee still.

Byron was, for most of his relatively short life, a poetic adventurer and a very adventurous poet. He had become Lord Byron, the 6th Baron, as a boy when he was transformed from obscure poverty by inheriting his peerage – and some wealth to go with it – from his uncle, his father having died earlier. As a boy he was awkward – he had a clubfoot – but extraordinarily handsome.

To less than universal acclaim he published his first poetry, *Hours of Idleness*, soon after he left school. But a wandering nature was soon apparent when he commenced a grand tour soon after his twenty-first birthday. He travelled widely and in 1811 returned to England to publish the first part of *Childe Harold*, a work which brought him almost instant recognition, fame and adoration. He had become firmly established.

He had many affairs, with both men and women, and shocked much of society at the time. He had a brief unhappy marriage which ended in separation in 1816. Disturbed and bitter, Byron left England to travel extensively in Switzerland and Italy where some of his most impressive poetry was written. He finished *Childe Harold*, and began his masterpiece *Don Juan* when in Venice. Partly spurned by British society, partly adored, he was never to return to his native land.

In 1823, at the age of thirty-five, from across the Adriatic he observed Greece, ancient birthplace and home of poetry, and became obsessed with it. He adopted the Greeks' struggles for independence from the Ottoman Empire and decided to throw all he had into their cause.

Welcomed by the Greeks he went to live in Missolonghi where he and his money were at their disposal in their war. It was here that his health began to deteriorate. He had never been very fit and in April 1824 he caught a fever and died the day after Easter on 19 April.

Despite his wish to buried in Greece they took his body home to England and he was buried with huge, if lonely, ceremony in Nottinghamshire. His lungs had been removed and left *in memoriam* with the citizens of Missolonghi.

–

Byron's death was received back in Britain with a wave of sadness for this romantic, tragic star. It increased the British people's sympathy for the cause of Greek independence. Greece declared him a national hero and proclaimed him a 'father and benefactor of the nation'. Generally 'scandalous', very talented but above all a definite romantic, Byron has never been equalled. His struggle for a nation's freedom and the freedom of his poetry made him unique.

19 The LAST mantraps

1827

The illicit killing of game for food was once the subject of a very severe set of game laws in Britain. A capital offence in the 18th century, in the 1820s armed poaching was still punished with transportation. The magistrates in the courts which enforced these laws were very often the same landowners on whose land the poaching was discovered.

As for shooting game, even with the landowner's permission, this could still be a serious offence. Only 'esquires' or gentlemen of senior rank, and their eldest sons, could legally use a shotgun to shoot for sport.

One of the more vicious methods of deterring the poacher was the use of man-traps. These were similar in principle to a mousetrap. Chained in place on the ground, hidden in the undergrowth, a large pair of metal jaws with jagged interlocking teeth was held open, waiting for its victim. The jaws were spring-loaded and anyone stepping onto a metal plate was immediately clamped in a dreadful grip. Broken limbs and permanent injury were usually the result.

To the dismay of the rich landowners who suffered from poaching, Robert Peel's law reforms made the use of man-traps illegal – they were last used legally in Britain in 1827.

–

The serrated jaws of these devices for maiming the unsuspecting trespasser are, today, a great favourite in 'black' museums.

20 The LAST fleet action under sail

20 October 1827

The Battle of Navarino is notable for two things: the utter confusion during the course of fighting and the fact that it was the last naval fleet engagement to be fought wholly under sail.

On one side were the ships of Britain, France and Russia. They were mediating in the Greek War of Independence, where Turkey and its ally Egypt were engaged in fighting the Greeks.

The fleets of the three Western Allies had joined together in October 1827 to form a squadron under the command of Trafalgar veteran, Vice-Admiral Sir Edward Codrington. He had ten ships-of-the-line, ten frigates, one corvette and some half-dozen schooners at his command. The Turkish commander, Ibrahim Pasha, had his combined fleet of well over sixty-five ships anchored in a large semi-circle in Navarino Bay, on the western edge of the Greek Peloponnese peninsula. Two large Turkish shore batteries provided protection. Ibrahim Pasha had agreed that he would not to leave the bay until the Turkish Sultan had responded to the Allies' mediation attempt.

Unfortunately a Greek naval division arrived in the nearby

Gulf of Patras and this was too much for Ibrahim Pasha. He made two attempts to send some of his fleet to intercept them. These were turned back by the Allies. On land the Turkish army was busy attacking the Greeks. Codrington decided to intervene directly with a show of force which he hoped would induce Pasha to desist.

On 20 October he ordered his squadron to enter the bay and moor alongside the Turkish and Egyptian ships. With his flagship *Asia*, 80 guns in the lead, this operation began. Initially there was no reaction.

It was only when the British frigate *Dartmouth* was sent to warn off some Turkish fireships and was attacked that the battle began. Gradually, as ship after ship on both sides started to engage its nearest enemy the bay was engulfed in gunfire and smoke.

The shore batteries opened up on the French ships as the Russian ships, with wind dropping, struggled to reach their positions alongside the enemy. Visibility, as usual in these affairs, was poor. Most of the ships' crews had great difficulty in seeing their neighbours. However, before moving into the bay, one of Codrington's instructions to all his squadron had been, in imitation and no doubt admiration of his old commander Nelson's words 'If a general action should take place, no captain can be better placed than when his vessel is alongside one of the enemy.' This duly happened and despite the overwhelming superiority in numbers of Ibrahim Pasha's fleet, the Western Allies' ships and men gave an excellent account of themselves. Many ships caught fire. After about two hours of close-quarter battle, most of the Turkish ships were either ablaze or blown up and sunk.

According to Codrington's despatches the enemy, 'out of a fleet composed of 81 men-of-war, only one frigate and 15 smaller vessels are in a state ever to be again put to sea.' Despite this, most of the British ships and all of the French had to return to home ports for repairs.

The Allies' casualties were, however, light: 150 killed and less than 500 wounded. In the days when the crews for even the smaller ships were numbered in hundreds, when they were subjected to cannon and grape shot, musket fire, grenade explosions and vicious wood splinters for several hours, these numbers would have been regarded as acceptable.

The British Government were unsure how to react to their victory. None of the countries concerned was actually at war.

Codrington was, for a short time recalled home in disgrace.

Navarino was an accident of arms that should never have happened. Britain's Navy was regarded as supreme and had seldom been challenged after the defeat of the French in 1815. Throughout most of the 19th century only relatively small naval skirmishes occurred. The Royal Navy had to wait until the Battle of Jutland in the First World War for its next full fleet action. By then the 'wooden walls of England', driven only by sails, had given way to the steam power of the dreadnought battleships.

21 The LAST official Catholic discrimination

18 May 1832

Religious liberty has only been grudgingly granted to British citizens. The freedom to practise virtually any religion was however established by the the 18th century but bigotry was still rife. Open discrimination, particularly against Catholics, was quite legal. The ultimate test of full citizenship however was regarded as whether any person could become a member of Parliament. In 1829 Daniel O'Connell was the last Christian to be barred from Parliament for refusing, as a Roman Catholic, to take the oath of supremacy.

In 1828 the Test and Corporation Acts had been abolished. These laws had required official oaths from those taking up various public offices which effectively disqualified anyone who was not a member of the protestant Church of England. Many exceptions had been allowed to these laws, framed in the time of King Charles II, to allow almost all protestants – dissenters included – to take part in public life. So their repeal merely cleared up the law as was then practised.

At this same time Catholic emancipation was the real issue of the day and it was being fought out in the towns and villages of Catholic Ireland. The Duke of Wellington as Prime Minister was eventually forced to deal with this near intractable problem.

The Catholic Association, led by the Roman Catholic priesthood and with Daniel O'Connell as its main spokesman, was in a very strong position and agitating for the right for Catholics to sit in Parliament. In county Clare, in a Parliamentary by-election, O'Connell, a Catholic and thus disqualified from taking his seat, stood against Vesey Fitzgerald who was offering himself for re-election as he had just accepted a Government post. O'Connell won and set in action a series of events that were very swiftly to lead to Catholic emancipation.

The agitation in Ireland grew worse. To the alarm of the Government, it spread to England where open conflict and cries of 'no popery' were increasingly heard. The Government soon admitted the justice of the Catholics' cause and that nothing short of full emancipation would satisfy them. Action was needed quickly to avoid prolonged demonstrations and dangerous conflict.

The Duke of Wellington was a realist. Although personally against the measure he and his ministers, namely Robert Peel as Home Secretary, accomplished a *volte-face* and brought in legislation for 'Catholic relief'. This altered the oath of allegiance to the Church of England required of all members of Parliament. An amazing amount of hard work was required to persuade his Tory party to support the measure, the House of Lords to approve it and the King not to obstruct it. The job was eventually done in April 1829.

On 15 May O'Connell arrived at the House of Commons to take his seat. As he had been elected under the old rules the clerk presented him with the old oath which included a denial of fundamental Roman Catholic beliefs and a declaration of the supremacy of the sovereign in all religious matters. He refused and from the bar of the House argued his case. The debate continued on the 18 May, but after a long and very eloquent statement the use of the new oath was again refused to O'Connell. He returned to Dublin to a very enthusiastic reception from his supporters who knew that the case was all but won. A triumphal progress to Clare was followed by his decisive re-election for the seat on 30 July. He was duly sworn in under the new oaths and at last took his seat in Parliament.

A significant side issue to this legislation was that it now allowed Roman Catholic peers to enter Parliament. There were eight English, twelve Irish and two Scottish lords who were immediately enabled to take their seats in Parliament in the Upper House.

—

And so, in the United Kingdom, *official* concern at 'popery', in the form of open discrimination against Roman Catholics, drew to an end by their being allowed into Parliament. The Jews had to wait another thirty years before they were granted the same right.

22 The LAST of the body snatchers

1832

Great advances were being made in the study of medicine at the beginning of the 19th century. To achieve this, the surgeons needed a large supply of human bodies to dissect and on which to demonstrate their theories. These were supplied by body snatchers, or 'resurrectionists' as they were called, who dug up freshly buried corpses and sold them to the medical schools. The bodies of many executed criminals went the same way. The practice of body snatching rapidly died out in 1832 when a more reliable supply of bodies from the poor houses was provided by Act of Parliament.

When paupers faced death one of their greatest fears was not the certain unmarked grave that was to be their lot but the almost certain journey for their corpses, after burial, to the dissection tables in nearby schools of anatomy. They had a very firm conviction that the proper manner in which to meet their Maker was in one single piece.

Those with wealth could go to their deaths in peace, knowing that their graves would be protected and defended, at least for the first few weeks – after that the growing putrefaction of the corpse was its best and lasting protection.

The resurrectionists made their living by digging up recently buried bodies and selling them to the medical schools. This was quite legal as, according to law, the bodies were not actually owned by anyone. The shrouds, coffins and any clothing however was personal property and this could not be taken. At the dead of night the body snatchers would approach the graveyards looking for signs of freshly dug graves. With wooden shovels to deaden the noise the grave would be dug up, the body removed and the grave refilled.

The fresher and younger the corpse the more it could be sold for. A corpse with its full set of teeth was also highly prized as the teeth could be removed and sold separately for use as false teeth by the rich.

Burke and Hare were perhaps the most infamous of the body snatchers, if not quite the last. Unfortunately for their victims, and ultimately for themselves, they bypassed that part of the process which involved digging up the graves of the naturally departed. Impatient and greedy, they took to strangling the poorer clients in Hare's lodging house and selling the bodies to Dr Knox, a famous Edinburgh surgeon. They were eventually apprehended in 1829. Hare turned king's evidence to get off scot-free, but Burke was hanged and, in a most appropriate and fitting end, his body ended up under the dissectionist's knife.

The medical profession however was severely tainted by body-snatching. So, to protect their reputation, rather than the feelings and susceptibilities of the poor, the Cadaver Act was passed in 1832 which gave legal access to any unclaimed corpses of paupers from the poor houses and jails.

Once again, however, it was the poor who felt stigmatised, but it did stop body snatching and brought midnight peace once again to the graveyards.

–

With the new and assured supply of cadavers the study of anatomy thrived, prospered and developed. This led to the success of detailed and complicated internal surgical operations in the 1850s and 1860s which in turn did so much to establish the high reputation of Scottish and English surgeons that endures to this day.

23 The LAST of the rotten boroughs

June 1832

The representation in Parliament of the towns and shires of Britain was developed over several centuries. Never democratic

in the modern sense, the system had, by the 1800s, become obviously unequal and notoriously unfair. Pressure for change grew; the Parliamentary battles over the Great Reform Bill, attempting to abolish the 'pocket' and 'rotten' boroughs, were a nationwide sensation that lasted for more than two years.

Large areas of the country, such as Birmingham, Britain's second city, were completely unrepresented in Parliament. Other areas, whose populations had dwindled to mere handfuls, were over-represented, the infamous rotten boroughs. Bute in Scotland had only twelve voters; Old Sarum in Wiltshire had just seven; Dunwich in East Anglia, which had been swallowed up by the advances of the North Sea, still loyally returned two members to the House of Commons every election.

Voting was based on the ownership of the land; a pocket borough was 'in the pocket' of a rich landowner who could, if he owned enough of the land, literally and legally own a majority of the votes required to elect the member of Parliament. Seats in Parliament were openly bought and sold. Selling prices as high as £7,000 were recorded. Many important landowner peers each controlled several seats in the House of Commons.

The franchise, those entitled to vote, was also very small; only twenty-two seats out of over 600, had an electorate of more than a thousand; most had less than 500 – this usually to elect two or more members of Parliament. Among the voters there were no women, no working class, not even what today would be called the middle classes. In addition, with no secret ballot the practice of open bribery was common.

By the beginning of the 19th century there had developed considerable pressure to bring this corrupt system to an end. The prosperous, respectable middle classes wanted their share of power. The working classes were bitter and angry; they too wanted change – they talked of violence and seemed prepared to use it. Reform however was not a foregone conclusion; it was fiercely resisted, especially by the old Tories with their belief in property and even by the Church which saw a threat to its view of the established order of society.

The Duke of Wellington, who was Prime Minister in 1830, dug in his heels. He could envisage no useful improvements to the current political system. He said that 'beginning reform is beginning revolution' and believed that in a reformed Parliament no 'real

49

gentleman' would be able to take any further part in public affairs.

As Wellington and the Tories refused to tackle the reform issue, the King, William IV, reluctantly called on the Whig leader Earl Grey to form an administration and carry through the necessary legislation. Earl Grey appointed his Paymaster-General, Lord John Russell ('Lord' was a courtesy title as he was the younger son of the Duke of Bedford) to lead the Whigs in the House of Commons. So began the battles over the Great Reform Bill.

The Bill planned to sweep aside 143 rotten boroughs and to give the large towns and cities of the Midlands their own members of Parliament for the first time. It also proposed to increase the number of voters by using various different property qualification schemes. At the first attempt, in the House of Commons, the Bill understandably foundered – it had, after all, at least 143 self-interested opponents! Grey asked the King for a dissolution and an election on the single issue of Parliamentary reform followed. The Tories were trounced. When the Bill reached the House of Lords it was rejected; the battle shifted back to the Commons. The Bill was presented to the House for the third time by the indomitable Russell and was passed by two to one. Back in the House of Lords in May 1832 it was rejected again.

The country was in an uproar. This single issue dominated political thought and talk throughout the land.

Grey approached the King again. He brought a more severe message. Grey needed the King to create enough friendly Whig Peers to ensure the smooth passage of the Bill – the King refused and asked Wellington to take on the job. The Duke became convinced that orderly Government would be impossible so the premiership was passed back to Grey.

This time the King was more amenable. The royal threat was enough and when the Bill was brought to the Lords again most of its opponents stayed away. The Bill became law in June 1832 amidst sensational scenes throughout the country. Detailed Scottish and Irish Bills followed in July and August.

–

So ended the rotten boroughs. Although the Great Reform Act was a genuine attempt to widen the franchise and bring an end to the corruption, it seems relatively tame today. Without secret voting, the very real influence of the large landowners still persisted in pocket boroughs; Britain had to wait another forty years for that

'Can that mean me?' A contemporary cartoon urges William IV to acknowledge popular demands. Although William had the support of many of the artistocracy in his resistance to the Whigs' reforms of the 1830s, he eventually gave in and agreed to changes in the voting system.

to be remedied with the secret ballot.

As for extending the franchise, the Act was a disappointment. Although another 300,000 middle class electors were brought onto the rolls, the working class were excluded. They turned to the radical chartist movement for help.

Even today, boroughs can still go 'rotten' when populations shift; regular Boundary Commission reports ensure that constituency boundaries are moved to maintain reasonably equitable Parliamentary representation.

24 The LAST gibbeting
1832

In the days when the capture and conviction of vicious criminals was less certain than today, those who were caught received particularly brutal and savage punishment. Even after death, a convicted highwayman was not left in peace. Gibbeting, the hanging of the body 'in chains' in full public view, was considered a useful deterrent to other would-be 'gentlemen of the road'.

Gibbets were the gallows from which the bodies of the dead villains were suspended. There were usually gibbets positioned by the sides of the roads where many of the crimes of murder and robbery were committed. A metal cage, usually in the shape of the human form, was locked around the body to secure (most of it) from souvenir hunters and to prevent its premature disintegration. Permanent gibbets, with their grisly displays, were common, especially on Hounslow Heath to the west of London, an area that suffered from a disconcerting crimewave of highway robberies and murder in the early part of the century.

The gibbets were useful landmarks and even appeared on maps. Despite the gruesome sights and smells of decomposing bodies, many of the travelling public treated them as common-place, as a reassuring sign of civilisation, of law and order and, perhaps, even of safety.

The last recorded instance of gibbeting in England occurred in 1832. James Cook, a bookbinder, had waylaid a Mr Paas to rob him. He beat him to death and then took the body home where he cut it into pieces and burned it to try to hide the evidence. He was apprehended, convicted, executed and hanged in chains at Aylestone in Leicestershire on a thirty-three foot high gibbet.

Two years later the practice of gibbeting was abolished by law, to the relief of many, to the dismay, no doubt, of some. William Ewart, a member of Parliament and active abolitionist was mainly responsible. Public executions in Britain however were to continue for many more years.

25 The LAST almanacs tax

1833

A patent of monopoly, granted in the time of James I, allowed only a single publisher in Britain, the Stationers Company, to produce and sell almanacs to the public. These books were issued yearly and contained a curious mixture of astrological jargon and useful statistics. The monopoly was successfully challenged in the 18th century but a severe tax was placed on each copy, which restricted their circulation. The tax was removed in 1833 causing an explosion of different publications of a new and very definitely improved kind.

Until 1833, there were only two 'almanacks' available to the British public. Anyone wishing to obtain normal calendar information such as tide charts, phases of the moon or any other similar statistics would have to pay 1s 10d, including 1s 3d tax, to buy a copy of either Moore's or Partridge's almanac. The reader would then have been hard-pressed to wade through the pages of mumbo jumbo, 'remarks on the Divisions of the Heavens, with Judgements of the Eclipses and Seasons, handled according to the Rules of the Ptolomean Astrology, with many other things relating to the Truth of Astrology, calculated for the Meridian of London.' They were produced on poor quality paper to keep the cost down and had small circulations. The revenue raised was hardly worth the bother of collecting it.

After the tax was abolished in 1833, over 200 different new

almanacs were published within a few years. Soon there were many millions of copies sold nationwide. They covered every conceivable specialised need. Perhaps the most well known almanac was Whitaker's. Although it was only first published in 1869, it soon developed into an indispensable book for every Victorian household. Other periodicals and newspapers began the tradition of giving away their annual diaries or calendars, with or without advertising, of the type that we know today.

26 The LAST British Empire slavery

28 August 1833

Slavery in its many legal forms, from feudal serfdom to the full blooded body-owning slavery of the colonial plantations, existed in Britain and its overseas Empire for many hundreds of years. In 1833, after a long campaign, led by William Wilberforce and Thomas Clarkson amongst others, all slaves in the British Empire were freed. The Government compensated their owners, in effect 'buying' them to free them.

In a famous court case in 1772 it had been ruled that slavery in Britain itself was illegal; nobody could be a slave when actually in the British Isles. For the abolitionists this was just the start.

Trading in slaves, for Britons, had been abolished in 1807 but those already enslaved in the British Colonies were still legally the possessions of their owners.

Britain's naval strength was used to enforce the trading laws and to capture ships carrying illicit cargoes of slaves from Africa across the Atlantic. But for as long as there was a legal basis for slavery to exist, the high profits of this trade made it inevitable.

In 1823, with a certain amount of pious hope, the Government announced that the colonial authorities in the West Indies should 'reform' the system of slavery. Abolition was still regarded as avoidable and slavery was defended in certain quarters as 'not only expedient for the good of the commonwealth and beneficial for the negro but also sacred, founded on the authority of the Bible.'

This cynical argument grew fainter and by the time of the

Slaves celebrate their new freedom in
Barbados in 1834 as dispossessed
owners look on. The generous
compensation that owners received
for the loss of their 'property' went
some way towards allaying their
fears about negro emancipation.

reforming Whig Government of the 1830s Wilberforce and his friends found that their time had at last come – public opinion and the arguments from the intelligentsia were behind them.

Legislation was introduced in Parliament which included the sum of £20 million to compensate the owners for the loss of their property, the argument being that the law had sanctioned slavery – indeed had encouraged it – and that now it would be unjust to ruin financially the plantation owners over this matter. The British taxpayer, it turned out, was quite willing to pay this sum as the price of 'negro emancipation'.

There were few to oppose the Bill as it proceeded through Parliament and on 28 August 1833 the King gave it his royal assent despite his own personal opposition. Wilberforce had died a month before but he died knowing that his great cause had succeeded. The law came into effect a year later on 1 August 1834.

A complicated system of transferring slaves to a temporary bonded apprentice scheme was part of the Act. Some colonies accepted the spirit of the Act and by-passed the apprenticeships to give their slaves full freedom at once. Other colonies, in a different spirit, treated the apprenticed negroes even more harshly than before. Whatever the variations, by 1 August 1838 all slavery in the Empire was abolished. The one exception was Mauritius in the Indian Ocean where the authorities had to be prodded into action by the British Government.

Despite the gloom from the plantation owners in the West Indies, the economic disaster that they had predicted was avoided. Their trading, on the whole, continued to flourish.

One of the outcomes of the emancipation was the 'Great Trek' in South Africa. The Dutch settlers, unhappy with British rule anyway, had a very different kind of slavery. Their black native slaves, despite their lowly status, were treated almost as household servants. The monetary compensation was considered inadequate and the Dutch farmers voted with their feet. Over the next few years, in great ox wagon convoys, they moved out of the Cape of Good Hope, to settle in the north, in Natal on the east coast and across the Orange and Vaal rivers.

Over the next fifty years the rest of Europe and America followed Britain in the emancipation of slaves. The attitude of all the European countries to Africa, once dominated by the issue of slavery, now changed. Colonisation and the opening up of the 'dark continent' proceeded apace.

—

Slavery is still reputed to exist today in some of the more remote parts of the world. But it is internationally outlawed and no reputable bodies are able any longer to claim economic justification in its defence.

27 The LAST of the Royal Menagerie

1834

In the 18th century, as today, the Tower of London was one of London's top attractions for visits from the public. Along with the Royal Mint, the crown jewels and the very impressive collection of weapons and armour on display there was a fascinating menagerie, the Royal Menagerie no less, housing one of the finest collections of wild animals in Europe. As standards and expectations improved the animals at the Tower were moved to the newly opened Zoological Gardens in Regents Park and the Royal Menagerie finally closed in 1834.

The first record of a Royal Menagerie is in the time of Henry III when the gift of three leopards from Germany's Frederick II first established the collection of wild animals in the Tower. Soon there were other noble wild animals: lions and elephants drew amazed crowds from all over London and beyond.

The animal collection grew and of course was continually being replaced with newer and more exotic creatures for the sovereign's court to amuse itself with. Many of the animals were used in entertainment, in particular the bears for bear-baiting. The big wild cats intrigued the courtiers and they tested their ferocity by pitting tigers and lions against each other or by arranging for packs of dogs to be mauled by them.

But fashions and fashionable entertainments change and by the early part of the 19th century the royal collection at the Tower had dwindled to a few flea-bitten creatures hardly worthy of the name. A new Royal Keeper, Alfred Copps, was appointed in 1822 and he set about restoring the menagerie's reputation. Within a few years there were more than fifty different species of wild animal including an Indian elephant, an alligator and many snakes from all over the world. The collection exceeded its former glory.

On the other side of London however, in Regents Park, a new kind of animal collection was rapidly being gathered together. The Zoological Society of London was founded in 1826 by Sir Stamford Raffles. Within two years it was opened to the public and became a great success. There had been another royal animal collection at Windsor Castle and this was transferred to the Regents Park 'Zoo' around 1830. It seemed then by far the most logical place to keep wild animals. The process of transferring the animals from the Tower started in 1832. A lion attacked and badly injured one of the garrison in the Tower and the process was hurriedly completed. In 1834 the Royal Menagerie closed forever.

–

In Regents Park the tradition of keeping wild animals for amusement, for fascinating the public and even for scientific study continued. In Britain the tradition, started by royalty many years before, was now firmly in the hands of the 19th century scientists and philanthropists.

28 The LAST government dismissed by a monarch

14 November 1834

The development of the unwritten British Constitution over several centuries gradually took power away from the sovereign and, in theory at least, gave it to the people. One of the theoretical powers the sovereign still holds today, although not used, is that of being able to dismiss the Prime Minister and the Government of the day and ask another person to form an administration. The last monarch to dismiss a government, without consulting any other official source, was William IV in 1834.

After the passing of the first Reform Act by the Whigs, their leader Earl Grey eventually retired from public life. In the summer of 1834 the King, after his attempts to encourage a coalition ministry failed, reluctantly confirmed the Whigs in office and the premiership fell to Viscount Melbourne.

Melbourne was a skilled politician who gave the outward impression that he had no real political ambition. On receiving the invitation to become prime minister he described it as 'a damned bore', but he took the job nonetheless and was soon in conflict with his King over policy and appointments to the Government.

Lord Althorp was the Whigs' leader in the House of Commons, the continuation of which appointment had the King's approval. When Althorp, the son of an earl, succeeded to his father's earldom and moved to the House of Lords, Melbourne wished to replace him in the Commons with Russell.

Lord John Russell was a rising star in the Whig hierarchy. Unfortunately the King loathed him and found his insistence on the reform of the established Anglican Church in Ireland completely unacceptable. The King on this matter, as on most, wished it to be left well alone.

On Althorp's retirement from office the King genuinely expected Melbourne to resign too; he did not. On 14 November, after calling on the King at Windsor, Melbourne was handed a formal letter. The letter was polite and firm: he was dismissed.

Melbourne too was polite and uncomplaining. His attitude can best be summed up in his own later comment, 'I have always thought complaints of ill-usage contemptible, whether from a seduced disappointed girl or a turned out Prime Minister.' He even offered to carry any letter to the Duke of Wellington who was to be invited with Sir Robert Peel to form a Tory administration.

The press and the rest of Melbourne's cabinet were not so sanguine. There was astonishment and a strong disbelief the the King could have dismissed a Government which had such a large working majority in the House of Commons. The new administration which Peel put together was, by March the following year, reeling from a succession of defeats in Parliament. Peel almost begged the King to be released. To much relief all round, even to the King, Melbourne was called back and in April agreed to form his new ministry.

It is ironic, but somehow eminently suitable, that it was Melbourne who did so much to help the young Queen Victoria firmly onto the path of genuine constitutional monarchy a few years later.

29 The LAST bear-baiting

1835

Of all the sports involving animals, bear-baiting was certainly one the more cruel spectacles indulged in by the British public. A tethered bear would be set upon by a pack of dogs for the amusement of the crowd and bets were taken as to the fates of selected animals in the contest. It was an extremely popular sport throughout Europe from the middle ages onwards. In the early part of the 19th century the public conscience was at last pricked and in 1835 the sport was declared illegal.

Bear-baiting was one of those sports which attracted huge crowds whether at custom-built bear-baiting rings or at travelling fairs. A bear would first be chained to a post and goaded into anger by being whipped and taunted. A number of dogs would then be set on it and the crowd would watch the fun. During the fight bets were taken on which dogs would be the first – or the last – to die. In later years the bears were muzzled to prolong the spectacle and give the dogs more of a chance. Sometimes the bear would be killed, sometimes it would survive. Both the bears and the dogs were specially bred for the purpose.

This circus would not only appear at regular 'bear gardens' in the cities but would also tour from fair to fair, in different towns and villages.

The sport had a long, almost reputable history. Henry VIII for instance had a special bear-baiting ring built at Southwark in south London. His daughter Elizabeth I also enjoyed the contests.

Banning the sport was tried many times by various groups. The puritans abhorred the sport, 'not', it was said, 'because it gave pain to the bear, but because it gave pleasure to the spectators.' Nonetheless public opinion did at last swing from such bloody affairs. In 1835 a law was passed which made bear-baiting, and all similar sports such as bull-baiting, illegal.

–

Bear-baiting continued illegally for some years, but in public the practice was over. Very few fights took place after the 1850s. The British public gradually came to think that delight in watching pain being inflicted on other creatures was one of its less desirable attributes. It submitted to the civilising influence of the regulation and eventual banning of this kind of sport. Today, blood sports of various kinds still continue although no fighting against tethered animals is permitted.

30 The LAST inland waterways

1835

The 18th century saw a rapid expansion of the inland waterway system throughout Britain. The roads had been quite unsuitable for heavy loads and constant traffic so the canals were developed as the very sinews of industry. Without them neither the raw materials nor the finished products of the Industrial Revolution would have reached their destinations.

By the 1830s however the railways were doing to the canals what they were also doing to the roads – 'railroading' them off the map. The last major inland waterway to be constructed in Britain was the Birmingham and Liverpool Junction Canal in 1835.

The Chester canal system was isolated from the main canals around the 'engine room of industry', Birmingham. In an Act of Parliament of 1826 permission was given to build a canal to join the two systems. The most famous engineer of his day, Thomas Telford, was hired to build it. It ran for forty miles, much of it in a straight line, from Autherley Junction near Birmingham north to Nantwich. It had twenty-six narrow locks and one short tunnel and was opened in 1835 a few months after Telford's death. It cost £16,000 per mile to build.

It was not long before the financial power of the railways was felt by the canal companies. The canals had had their own way for many years, holding a virtual monopoly in transport. The railways broke that monopoly and received much support for doing so. Ironically the canals were used to transport much of the material required to build the railways. The railway companies then bought them out and often used the actual canal routes on which to lay more tracks.

The Birmingham and Liverpool Junction Canal was taken over

by the Ellesmere and Chester Canal Company and then almost immediately, in 1846, this was bought out by a new company, the Shropshire Union Railways and Canal Company, formed to exploit both canals and railways.

The Manchester Ship Canal was opened in 1893, but being designed for sea-going ships, it was not, strictly speaking, an inland waterway. Although many of the canals continued to operate effectively – the system was maintained, modernised and in some cases further extended – no new major inland canals were built in Britain after 1835. And so it proved that Telford's last canal was the beginning of the end for the inland waterways. Today, very few are used for commercial transportation but many miles have been successfully restored for pleasure cruising, including Telford's Birmingham and Liverpool Junction.

31 The LAST Hanoverian kings

20 June 1837

When Queen Anne died in 1714 without living descendants the Stuart line, so far as it was recognised in Britain, died with her. The British line of succession passed to the descendants of Elizabeth Stuart, daughter of James I. Elizabeth Stuart's daughter Sophia had married the German Ernest Augustus, ruler and Elector of Hanover. Sophia, the Electress of Hanover, had been declared Anne's heir but died just a few months before her. Her son 'German George' succeeded to the throne as George I. Along with his entire German entourage, he brought to the British crown the name and hereditary Electorship of Hanover.

The Hanoverian Dynasty ruled Great Britain for over a hundred years. Each Hanoverian monarch was also Elector of Hanover until 1814, when Hanover itself became a kingdom. The British king at the time, the mad King George III, thus became King of Hanover too.

William IV was the last of the Kings of Hanover on the British throne. He disliked the place and one of his younger brothers, Adolphus, Duke of Cambridge, had ruled there on behalf of the

British kings, since the early part of the century. William, the 'sailor' king, died on 20 June 1837. The British crown passed to his young niece, Victoria, but the Hanoverian crown was governed by Salic law which debarred inheritance through the female line. Thus the next King of Hanover was another of Victoria's uncles, one of William IV's other younger brothers, the eccentric, bombastic and mischievous, Ernest Augustus, Duke of Cumberland.

Thus William IV was not only the last of the male Hanoverians on the British throne (Victoria was a Hanoverian too) but he was also the last of the Kings of Hanover on the British throne.

–

Ernest died in 1851 and was succeeded as King of Hanover by George V. He was the last king. He died in 1866 and that same year Hanover was annexed by Prussia.

32 The LAST Martello towers

1837

Permanent fortifications in the shape of the squat round 'Martello' towers have been prominent landmarks on many parts of the British coastline ever since the Napoleonic wars. The last one to be built in the British Isles was in Jersey in 1837.

The name Martello comes from a typically British corruption of a foreign word. A fortified Mediterranean watch tower at *Mortella Point* in Corsica so impressed some Royal Navy officers and British engineers who had been sent to capture it that the design was later copied all around Britain when Napoleon's invasion threat was at its height.

The idea was that a series of 'Corsican' or Martello towers – strategically positioned – would keep a heavily armed naval force at bay for an indefinite period. Such a simple idea seems obvious but at the time the notion that anything could resist a broadside from a modern 74-gun battleship, the supreme fighting machine of the early 19th century, was hard to imagine. But experience at Mortella Point had proved it; so work began to defend the coastline from the attentions of the over-confident 'Boney' and his 'Army of England' in Boulogne just a few miles across the English Channel.

In the period of the war with France, nearly 200 towers were built, mostly around Britain although some were as far afield as the Cape of Good Hope and North America.

The main features of the Martello tower were its thick stone walls and its single entrance well above ground level. The design evolved and changed over the years and was adapted to local materials and conditions; they were usually constructed in local stone and about forty feet high. Thicker at the base than at the top, the ground level diameter was about 45 feet. The towers were armed with a few relatively light guns and could be manned by a handful of men.

They were never used in anger: the French and Spanish Fleets were destroyed at Trafalgar in 1805 and without them an invasion of Britain was impossible.

After the war with France ended in 1815 Martello building on mainland Britain ceased. A reappraisal of the defences of the Channel Islands however, in the new era of steam-driven ships, brought about the need for some new fortifications on Jersey. Five were planned and built in the 1830s, the last being on the east of the island, overlooking the bay of Petit Portelet. It was named *Victoria* in honour of the new young queen who had just ascended the throne. Martello building continued further afield however, the very last being started, but never finished, in Florida in 1873.

–

Victoria, along with many of its contemporaries, still stands today. Some towers have been restored and are now permanent memorials of defences that were never used. Like their more recent counterparts, the second World War 'pill boxes' that are still dotted about the English landscape, the Martellos can still be regarded as part of a very successful deterrent strategy.

33 The LAST pillory

1837

The public pillory, a wooden frame in which petty criminals could be locked, was once widely used throughout Britain. The public humiliation received by the offenders sentenced for a

Despite the fact that the pillory was
used for punishing relatively minor
offences, some of its victims died
under hails of missiles from
bystanders and from physical attacks
by the excitable crowds. Among
many other reforms of the legal
system the use of the pillory was
abolished in 1837.

day in the pillory was their punishment. The pillory was last officially used in Britain in 1837.

There were pillories and stocks erected in many public places. Every ward in London, for instance, had its stocks to deal with 'vagabonds and other petty offenders' at the end of the 16th century. The pillory, and the associated stocks, were used as one of the simpler methods of punishment. The writer Daniel Defoe was one of the pillory's more famous victims early in the 18th century when he suffered a spell in the pillory for publishing a libelous essay.

The hapless offenders were clamped in these frames: in the pillory by their necks and arms; in the stocks by their legs and sometimes their necks. In this position, they were at the mercy of the passing crowd. Sometimes the treatment they received was a mild affair. Missiles such as rotten fruit and perhaps a few nastier items of refuse were thrown at the victims – and with these attentions they came to no real harm. On other occasions the mob was stirred to real anger – perhaps because the crime was worthy of it or perhaps the crowd were bored and wanted some cruel fun. In these cases, those in the pillory could be seriously injured.

—

In line with many other civil and legal reforms of the 1830s the pillory was abolished by statute in 1837. Today, we can chuckle at the sight of the stocks – as museum pieces – on the older market squares and village greens and forget the grim, cruel side to history that once required their real use.

34 The LAST change in the royal coat-of-arms

1837

The coat-of-arms of the British royal family has changed many times since Richard the Lionheart adopted the lions of England as his emblem in the 12th century. The last change occurred when Victoria ascended the throne in 1837 and the shield representing the Kingdom of Hanover was omitted.

Claims to different kingdoms, England, Scotland, Ireland and particularly France, have played an important part in the design of the British royal Coat-of-arms through the centuries. In addition, the Hanoverian kings had brought with them to the British throne the lands of German Hanover. An escutcheon (a smaller shield within the larger shield) on the British royal coat-of-arms displayed the Hanoverian coat-of-arms, the two lions of Brunswick, the rampant lion of Luneburg and the famous white horse of Hanover, capped with the crown of Charlemagne. This escutcheon was dropped when Queen Victoria ascended the throne as, due to Salic law, she did not succeed to the Kingdom of Hanover.

Today the royal coat-of-arms indicates only wholly legitimate claims and is unchanged from Victoria's. The shield consists of four 'quarters' on which are the devices of the different kingdoms of the United Kingdom. 'England' in the first and fourth quarters, 'Scotland' in the second quarter and 'Northern Ireland' in the third quarter. Wales, a principality not a kingdom, is not represented.

'England' in heraldic language is described as: *Gules three Lions passant guardant Or, armed and langed azure* (three golden lions, each with blue claws and tongue, on a red background). 'Scotland' is: *Or a Lion rampant within a double tressure, flory counterflory Gules* (a red lion, standing on its hind legs, on a gold background inside a double border decorated with fleur-de-lys). 'Northern Ireland' is: *Azure a Harp Or stringed Argent* (a golden harp with silver strings on a blue background).

In Scotland the royal Coat-of-arms gives priority to the Scottish single lion rampant, it being placed in the first and fourth quarters and 'England' taking up only one quarter, the second.

When Queen Victoria married Prince Albert in 1840 she so adored him that she must have forgotten all the normal royal heraldic rules. She requested that the shield of her coat-of-arms should be quartered with those of her beloved Albert. She was very annoyed when reminded that, unlike other coats of arms, hers symbolised the realms over which she ruled and not family alliances or other minor dynastic details.

A change now in the royal coat-of-arms will occur only if there is a significant change in the status of the United Kingdom of Great Britain and Northern Ireland.

35 The LAST 'Constable'

1837

John Constable was one of the giants of the British painting world in the first part of the 19th century. His landscapes influenced even the French painters of the period. Constable's last painting was *Arundel Mill and Castle* painted in 1837.

The look and feel of Constable's paintings can be summed up no better than with his own words 'The sound of water escaping from mill-dams, willows, old rotten planks, slimy posts, and brickwork, I love such things. . . those scenes made me a painter and I am grateful.'

The English countryside, particularly Suffolk, was immortalised by his *Flatford Mill* and *Hay Wain*, known to millions of people as the peaceful rural epitomes of their age.

Towards the end of his life he was very taken with the beauty and majesty of Arundel Castle. He wanted it to influence his work, to provide less of the picturesque and more of the beautiful things of life, to give it a new 'broken ruggedness' as he called it.

–

Arundel Mill and Castle which he was working on when he died in 1837 retains both the picturesque and the beauty of life and now hangs in the Toledo Museum of Art in the USA.

36 The LAST battle on British soil

31 May 1838

John Nicholl Thom was a doomed eccentric, too bizarre a character even for Britain in the early 19th century. Thom, who is credited with causing the last battle on British soil, died 'in action' on 31 May 1838.

John Thom was originally a corn merchant in Cornwall. Calling himself Count Moses Rostopchein Rothschild, he arrived in Kent in the early 1830s and began conducting campaigns against 'taxation, slavery, the primogeniture law, and chartered and corporate bodies.' He championed many other seemingly random causes and had soon re-styled himself 'Sir William Percy Honeywood Courtenay, Knight of Malta, Rightful Heir to the Earldom of Devon, King of the Gypsies, King of Jerusalem.' He also saw himself as the defender of the causes of rural workers and carried a large curved sword as his personal weapon.

'Sir William' rapidly gathered large numbers of supporters. So much so that the Tories invited him to stand for Parliament in Canterbury against the Whigs in 1833. He polled 950 votes but failed to be elected. He soon fell foul of the law. Convicted of perjury, he was sentenced to six years' transportation but this was commuted to a stay at Barming Lunatic Asylum, where he clearly belonged. In October 1837 he was released and it was not long before he was up to his old tricks.

He now proclaimed that he had a divine mission; in fact he announced himself to be the Messiah, 2,000 years old. He led a band of disaffected farm labourers who worshipped and did homage to him as their Saviour. As proof of his status he claimed to be invulnerable to shot and proved it by firing a supposedly fully loaded pistol into his own body.

He was soon wanted by the local justices. Hiding in a farm at Herne Hill, he was forced to withdraw into a nearby forest known as Bosenden Wood with forty of his gang after he shot and stabbed to death an unfortunate constable named Mears who was sent to arrest him.

Stationed at Canterbury were the 45th Regiment of Foot. A detachment of one hundred soldiers was despatched to deal with Sir William's now open revolt. They split into two groups to advance on Bosenden Wood. The rebels managed momentarily to keep the initiative when they surprised a small party of approaching soldiers. Sir William stepped forward, deliberately took careful aim and shot and killed the officer in charge, Lieutenant Bennett. Several other soldiers were wounded.

Battle proper then commenced. Armed with cudgels, knives, swords and pistols, the rebels fought off the much better equipped soldiers. Inevitably however, the rebels were outclassed and were soon overwhelmed. When the fighting was over eight rebels lay dead on the forest floor. Among the dead was Sir William. He was buried in an unmarked grave in the local churchyard – the part of the burial service referring to the resurrection being omitted to avoid any further misunderstanding from his followers. A guard was posted to see that his body was left undisturbed.

Of his supporters, three were sentenced to transportation and a further six to a year's hard labour.

–

Today Thom, or 'Sir William', is still remembered, even by the successor regiment to the 45th, the Worcester and Sherwood Foresters, who participated in the 150th anniversary ceremony dedicated to the very last battle on British soil.

37 The LAST Irish tithes

1838

At the beginning of the 19th century the Church still required tithes, or tenths of the produce of the land, to be paid to it. The Church concerned was, of course, the established Anglican Church of England.

Tithe payments to the Church of England, with a history going back several centuries, applied to all members of the agricultural community, whether Free Church or Anglican and, particularly provocatively in Ireland, to all Catholics.

In every Parish, a tenth of all the harvest was due to be paid to the local priest. Every tenth part of the grain and corn went off to be stored in tithe barns to be disposed of as the Church saw fit. Some members of the clergy were more rigorous than others in enforcing the tenant farmers to come forward with their due; but, however applied, the tithe system – hitting only certain parts of the community and supporting only the one established Church – was an obvious anomaly that had to be dealt with.

Unrest in the countryside, amongst farming communities as well as mill workers, hastened the demise of this outdated system of taxation.

Opposition to the tithes was best organised and, of course, most justified in Ireland. Daniel O'Connell, an Irish Catholic politician who had been able to enter Parliament in 1829 only after Catholic emancipation was at the forefront of the campaign.

The Irish 'tithe wars', as they became known, consisted of

widespread resistance to paying the tax. Tithe collectors were beaten up and sometimes murdered. Curfews were imposed all over Ireland and the military had to be called out to retain law and order.

When Lord Melbourne became Prime Minister in 1835 O'Connell struck a deal with him and finally in 1838 a law was passed which replaced the tithes with a rent charge for the land, payable by the landowner. This satisfied the strong grievances held by the Irish and immediately alleviated the problem.

–

A similar solution to the tithe problem had been applied in the rest of the United Kingdom two years earlier. Payments in kind were abolished, but the tenants were still responsible for making the payment. They had to wait until 1891 for the landlord to be made responsible. In 1936 the rent charges were phased out completely.

38 The LAST Bow Street Runners

1839

The policing of Britain's capital has always been a controversial role, sometimes achieved with honesty and vigour, sometimes less so. Magistrates and constables existed in plenty but justice was rough and their effectiveness usually patchy. By the beginning of the 19th century London had a number of official and semi-official groups for keeping law and order. Among the best known of these were the Bow Street Runners. They remained an active force until disbanded in 1839.

The Bow Street Runners, the first attempt at a regular London police force, had been created in 1750 by the writer Henry Fielding who was also a magistrate at Bow Street. At first the force was a small group of detectives pitted against the criminal gangs of London. Later, developed by Henry's brother John, they were enlarged and in 1805 a mounted patrol group was added to guard the public from the expanding activities of highwaymen in a twenty mile radius around the city.

They gained an admirable reputation for determination and incorruptibility. The criminals feared and respected them, as a highwayman's song of the period exclaims:

> I went to London one fine day
> With my sweet love to see the play,
> Where Fielding's gang did me pursue
> And I was ta'en by that cursed crew.

They continued to play a useful role in and around London for some years after the Metropolitan Police was created by Robert Peel in 1829. They were a curious mixture of a service – half private, half public – sometimes earning good money working for wealthy clients who required their specialised services.

They eventually disappeared in 1839, fully absorbed into the Metropolitan Police.

–

Today the memory of the Bow Street Runners lingers on. Bow Street Magistrates Court is still in use, dispensing justice for a large part of central London.

39 The LAST great auk

1840

Despite the ravages of man upon his environment, the British Isles have witnessed surprisingly few extinctions of animal species in recorded history. An exception to this was the demise of the great auk, a sea bird which finally disappeared in 1840.

The great auk, *alca impennis*, was a large flightless sea bird of the North Atlantic area. Extremely vulnerable to human attentions through its inability to fly, it resembled a huge razorbill. It existed in North America, Greenland, Iceland and northern Britain. When nesting it laid a single egg and lived on exposed cliff and coastal sites.

The last recorded breeding in the wild in Britain was in 1812 when a bird was seen on its nest in the Orkneys.

The species was eventually 'collected' and hunted to extinction in the British Isles when in 1840, the last specimen was killed on the island of St Kilda.

–

In Iceland the great auk struggled on. According to records, the last living specimen was killed in June 1844, the great auk now living on only in memories and watercolours.

40 The LAST steam omnibuses

1840

One of the most magnificent means of transport devised in the 19th century was the steam powered omnibus. Based on the horse-drawn coaches of the day, with the added touch of some brilliant engineering innovations that were far ahead of their time, they competed successfully with horse powered omnibuses and coaches. For a time also they threatened the 'invention of the century', the railways. Eventually however a combination of the railway companies' vested interests and the short-sightedness and conservatism of the Turnpike Trusts managed literally to drive the road steamers off the roads in 1840.

In 1801 a Cornishman named Richard Trevithick built the first successful steam carriage, but it had to wait twenty years to be developed into a reasonable commercial proposition. Sir Goldworth Gurney built a succession of steam powered coaches for Sir Charles Dance in the early 1820s. These road steamers incorporated a number of features such as speed changing gears, compensating steering geometry and the differential drive hub and back axle found in all road vehicles today. They were capable of over 10 miles per hour and they travelled the nine miles between Cheltenham and Gloucester with fare-paying passengers three times a day. Despite highly competitive prices Sir Charles's steamers were not the commercial success they should have been.

There was a deeply ingrained opposition to the steam carriages, mainly due to prejudice fuelled at every opportunity by the fast developing railway companies. Also, the roads at that time were not really capable of taking heavy traffic. Rather than improve the roads, the Turnpike Trusts put every obstacle in the way of steam road transport. The toll structures were deliberately set up to penalise the steamer, its toll being over ten times that for an ordinary horse drawn coach. This was despite the existence of more than adequate proof that a coach pulled by horses would actually cause more damage to a road surface than a steam carriage.

Then there was the fear of explosion of the steamers' boilers. This was very much exaggerated and in any case was no more likely to occur than on the railways.

Walter Hancock in London had more success. He set up the London and Paddington Steam Carriage Company in 1833 and ran a series of trial routes in London in his grandly, if obscurely, named vehicles *Enterprise* and *Autopsy*. He then travelled the country demonstrating the ability of his new vehicles.

Many other companies followed. In 1834 the Steam Carriage Company of Scotland began services between Glasgow and Paisley. It had six vehicles and for a number of years undertook the forty minute journey every hour throughout the day until sabotage put it out of business. In the same year Telford and Stephenson had given their backing to the London, Holyhead and Liverpool Steam Coach and Road Company. With remarkable foresight this company intended to address the real problem, the roads, by building and maintaining its own.

In London, Hancock held out longest against the opposition. His latest vehicle, the splendid *Automaton*, capable of 20 miles per hour, ran regularly for a number of years. Finally in 1840 it was withdrawn from service forever. It was the last road steamer in service.

The demise of the steam powered omnibus and the rise of the railway train was not inevitable. Had the proponents of road steamers managed to convince some really powerful and influential backers early enough, and had the Turnpike Trusts been more adventurous, history might have had a different story to tell about that curious invention, the railway.

–

Steam power on the roads was left to the plodding traction engines which in 1865 were further restricted, on poor roads, by the Red Flag Act which decreed a ponderous maximum speed of four miles per hour. In the 20th century a revival of interest in the idea showed that it was practicable when steam powered lorries ran successfully for many years before the Second World War.

Hancock's steam omnibus,
Automaton. Hancock ran services in
various parts of London for seven
years before his London and
Paddington Steam Carriage
Company folded in 1840, bringing the
adventure of passenger-carrying road
steamers to an end.

41 The LAST new-born heir

9 November 1841

Not many kings or queens of Great Britain were born directly as heir to the throne. Many were born as second or third in line, with one of the parents already the direct heir. Many others became the heir and succeeded only due to the death of a close relation. As longevity and the survival chances have increased from generation to generation, the likelihood of an heir being born in direct line of succession has receded.

The last truly 'majestic' birth, as far as the British crown is concerned, was that of Albert Edward, the Earl of Chester, heir and second child of Queen Victoria, the future Prince of Wales and King Edward VII. This momentous event took place in the morning of 9 November 1841 at Buckingham Palace. Up to that moment the heir to the throne was his one year old sister, Princess Victoria, whom he automatically replaced in the line of succession. Prince Albert Edward was christened in St George's chapel at Windsor Castle the following January. The Queen went on to give birth to another seven children, nine princes and princesses in all, seven of whom survived her. They married into many branches of the royal families of Europe.

–

After Edward VII, no British monarchs have been born first in line to the succession. Indeed, only one, Edward VIII, could, at the time of his birth, have been expected to reign at all. George V became king only because his elder brother Eddy had died earlier; and George VI and his daughter, the present Queen Elizabeth II, succeeded due to the abdication of the uncrowned Edward VIII, George VI's brother.

42 The LAST private lighthouse

26 July 1841

Today all British lighthouses, vital beacons for all navigators around the British Isles, are controlled by Trinity House, an ancient guild specially incorporated to do the job. This was not always so. Many lighthouses used to be run for private profit. The last of these to be transferred from private hands to Trinity House was the Skerries lighthouse, in 1841.

Lighthouses have a long history, going back to ancient times in the Mediterranean area. In Britain they date at least from Roman times; but it was in the 13th century that the first record exists of a 'Letter Patent', under the authority of the Great Seal of State, granting the right to set up and operate a lighthouse, the funding for which was to come from a tax imposed upon all ships entering or leaving the nearby harbour.

By the 16th century Trinity House was in existence, and one of its prime functions was to operate the lighthouses required for mariners to navigate the waters around the coast.

The first Trinity House lighthouse was at Lowestoft, but it did not have a monopoly on the business. Privately run lighthouses began around the same time. Some of these were held under licence from Trinity House and some were licensed directly from the State, either in perpetuity or under a renewable licence scheme.

The main financing of all the lighthouses, whether Trinity House or private, were the dues collected by commissioners who visited harbours with the appropriate letters of authority to collect money from the ships' captains – usually around 1d per ton – after entering harbour. This had to be paid before a ship's cargo could be registered at the Custom House. Similarly, before leaving harbour, the dues had to be paid again before clearance could be obtained.

Gradually the system was perfected, usually for the benefit of the operators of the lighthouses. Foreign shipping was charged double the fees that British ship owners had to pay. In 1819 the fees to foreign ships were reduced to those for British ships. Even so, full compensation was paid by the Government to the private lighthouse owners.

As lighthouses became more and more profitable, Trinity House ploughed their profits back into the organisation; and they had charitable and philanthropic commitments too. The private lighthouse owners had no such worries. Abuses abounded and despite paying large commissions to their collectors their profits soared. In the 1830s, the fourteen privately run lighthouses received as much income as all of the fifty-five lighthouse in the hands of Trinity House.

Eventually in 1843, a Select Committee of Parliament was set up to look into the matter and an Act of Parliament was passed which 'vested all lighthouses of England and Wales in the corporation of Trinity House and gave power to the corporation to purchase all lighthouses remaining in private hands.'

This purchase was to include a very generous allowance as compensation to the owners for loss of income.

Gradually Trinity House negotiated the licences, whether permanent or renewable, from the private lighthouse operators. The one which held out the longest and was thus the last to be taken over by Trinity House was the Skerries lighthouse on the north western tip of Anglesey in Wales.

It had been built in 1717 and initially had been a failure, as far as revenue-earning prospects were concerned. But with the explosive growth of the shipping business in nearby Liverpool, it began to develop as a very profitable operation later in the century. By the beginning of the 19th century it was bringing in over £12,000 per annum for its owner. Originally it had a coal fired light (burning some 80 tons of coal a year) but in 1804 it was converted to oil and its tower was extended.

The proprietor of the Skerries was Morgan Jones. He fought long and hard to retain his privileges of ownership, claiming that an Act of Parliament gave him the rights over the Skerries forever. He turned down offers from Trinity House for £260,000, £350,000 and £400,000 without ever naming his price. Eventually the matter went to court to be settled by jury. At Beaumaris, under the High Sheriff, on 26 July 1841 the Jones's executors (he had just died) settled for the enormous sum of £444,984 11s 3d, which was declared to be the purchase of twenty-two years of a net income of £20,042 per annum, a truly phenomenal sum in those days. It was the last such purchase by Trinity House and by far the largest.

Trinity House continues to serve the mariners around Britain today. The Skerries lighthouse is still there, in Anglesey, also still serving. Gleaming white with a broad red band, it was modernised in 1963 and is open to the public.

43 The LAST income tax free period
1842

This is not the story of the demise of income tax in Britain, but the occasion when the entire populace was last free from such a tax. In 1798 income tax, at a then shocking 2.5% (sixpence in the pound), was first introduced to the British people by Prime Minister Pitt to pay for the war against France. At the conclusion of the war it was – uncharacteristically one might think – removed, its *raison d'être* having disappeared.

But, as Benjamin Franklin had observed some years earlier, 'in this world nothing can be said to be certain except death and taxes', and, sure enough, in 1842 Britain's last period of income tax free existence came to an end.

Sir Robert Peel, with his free trade ideas, had set about rationalising the taxation system. These policies reduced the money for the exchequer from indirect taxes, such as customs duties, but increased it with direct taxes, such as that on income. When re-introduced, income tax applied only to those earning more than £150 a year – a considerable and comfortable income in those days. It was set at 7d in the pound (less than 3%). At first it was for a limited period of three years but it subsequently proved impossible to abolish. Many chancellors of the exchequer have tried – Gladstone reduced it to 2d – but it is still with us and has increased considerably over the years.

Thus ended those halcyon days when the rich managed to prevent any of their income ending up in the national purse.

–

In Britain the standard rate of income tax reached a peak of 50% during the Second World War but today it seems to be on its way down. There are some serious politicians who hope to see this most basic of all direct taxes disappear forever.

44 The LAST of the wreckers

23 October 1842

For centuries the normal dangers to ships' crews in coastal waters was added to by the possibility of being lured onto the rocks, wrecked and then robbed by the lawless inhabitants of the wilder coastal regions. Wrecking was, at the very least, the opportune arrival on the scene of a fresh wreck from which to plunder anything of value. It was considered a legitimate perk for those living near the shore. The last known instance of deliberate wrecking on British shorelines was in 1842 when the ship *William Wilberforce* foundered on the North Devon coast.

Tradition has it that wreckers on stormy nights would carry lanterns up to cliff tops to entice storm battered ships' captains to aim for them in the belief that they were entering a friendly harbour. A lantern tied to the tail of a donkey led along a cliff-top path would appear to a ship at sea to be the riding light of a ship safely at anchor. The captain would head for this apparition and before he could realise his mistake would find himself wrecked on the rocks.

Usually the wreckers were not outlaw bands of desperate cut-throats but local inhabitants who indulged in some brutal behaviour to supplement their income. They were prepared to murder an entire ship's crew as they stumbled ashore.

The wreckers would make their way through the surf to bludgeon any surviving crew members who got in their way and carry off the cargo and any valuable fittings they could find. Any sailors left in distress were left to the mercy of the tides and weather.

In practice wrecking was more often opportunistic than deliberate. The news of a wrecked ship would draw the locals for miles around. If they could get hold of any valuables before they were ruined or washed out to sea then they regarded it as fair game.

The *William Wilberforce*, a brig of 167 tons, was built in Canada in 1816. In 1842 she was heading for Ilfracombe in North Devon but the crew never made it. The ship was lured ashore at Lee, a small harbour a few miles from Ilfracombe, on the night of 23

October 1842. There was a raging sea combined with very high winds. The captain and his crew of five seamen were drowned and the locals knowingly put the incident down to wreckers.

The instances of proven deliberate wrecking were always rare. Any mysterious wreck – especially when a ship was lost with all hands – would be attributed, sometimes unfairly, to wreckers. As the forces of law and order spread to the more remote coasts, especially to prevent smuggling, instances of wrecking became rarer.

—

Strangely, the *William Wilberforce* was not a total wreck. She was bought by a local ship repairer who had her refloated and towed off the rocks. Seaworthy again within a few months, she made many more successful voyages carrying timber to America and the Mediterranean, eventually foundering and being totally wrecked off Portugal in 1856.

45 The LAST sale of a royal palace

1845

The British royal family have lived in many different palaces, the records stretching back for over a thousand years. Some residences no longer exist, whereas others, such as one of the very first, the Tower of London, are used to fulfil a major part in ceremonial life today. Perhaps the most exotic of all these palaces was the Brighton Pavilion. A gorgeous and extravagant folly, it had a short royal life, only properly lived in by George IV and his beloved mistress, Maria Fitzherbert.

Until it was bought in 1784 by the then Prince of Wales as a country retreat, the Brighton Pavilion was a small country house. It was extensively remodelled between 1815 and 1822; John Nash was the architect who, acting under the prince's instructions, created a half-Indian, half-Chinese *mélange* of a building. Cobbett described the domed roofs as a collection of 'Norfolk turnips'. It was last used as a royal residence by Queen Victoria and Prince Albert in 1845. Victoria found that she disliked Brighton and thought that the Pavilion itself was 'a strange, odd Chinese looking thing' – undoubtedly true.

Once Prince Albert saw it however, it was doomed. His tastes did not include the exuberant fantasies which the queen's uncle had developed to such startling effect.

The royal couple were soon fully involved elsewhere. They had bought the Osborne estate on the Isle of Wight and their time was filled with the rebuilding of this house. They did not neglect Buckingham Palace and Windsor Castle and, a few years later, energetic as ever, they fell in love with Balmoral Castle in Scotland

The happy couple never missed Brighton. In 1850, the Brighton Pavilion was the last palace to be sold by the British royal family. After hundreds of items of furniture and other *objets d'art* had been removed – some to other palaces, some to be sold – the Pavilion was bought by the Brighton Town Corporation for £60,000.

–

The Brighton Pavilion can be visited today. It is an extraordinary building, an outrageous but wonderful oriental fake with few Victorian pretensions, right in the centre of an English south coast seaside resort. It is best thought of as a monument to the more amusing – even respectable – side of 'Prinny' the Prince Regent, later King George IV.

46 The LAST of the Corn Laws

26 May 1846

For some they were an iniquitous attack on the poor, preventing them from eating cheaply, depriving them of their very bread; for others they were an essential bastion to protect the country from collapse, maintaining the proper balance of agriculture and prices. They were the Corn Laws, imposed by the British Government in 1815, and they taxed imported wheat and corn and maintained an artificially high price for the staple of the working classes – bread.

Eventually, in what was one of the biggest political campaigns in the first half of the 19th century, the Corn Laws were abolished, repealed in 1846 after a great deal of public excitement including rioting and public meetings around the country.

At the end of the Napoleonic wars, foreign imports of corn started to flood into Britain. The country's farming was in tatters after over twenty years of national conflict. So, to protect the farming interests of the politically powerful landowners, the Government imposed high duties on all imported corn through the Corn Laws. These laws prohibited the import of cheap foreign corn when the home produced price was high; it allowed imports only when the home price was low. These rules were modified later to allow imports to enter the country at any time so long as high duties were paid. All this resulted in a comfortably inflated price for all home producers of corn and a high price was demanded from everyone when they bought their bread.

The town dwellers, the manufacturers and traders, were bitterly opposed to the laws – in their own self-interest of course. With cheaper bread, the factory owners could get away with lower wages to their workers; with cheaper foreign food the ship owners could make more money by bringing their ships home from trips abroad with holds full of corn.

All was not well with the farmers either despite the price protection they enjoyed. They soon realised that with the price of bread being so high, the sales of their other food products slumped. Along with increased mechanisation leading to a requirement for fewer workers at lower wages, the high price of bread was the main cause of growing social unrest in the countryside.

In 1838 the Anti Corn Law League was founded. Two of its brightest stars were Richard Cobden and John Bright, both at various times members of Parliament. They used many campaigning methods that would be recognised and admired today. They lobbied members of Parliament, they held public meetings and, from 1840, they used the penny post to send campaigning leaflets to many voters all around the country. In effect a 'pressure group', they were eventually successful.

In 1845 famine hit Ireland a vicious blow. The potato crop failed and over three quarters of a million Irish peasants died in the harshest of conditions. Despite deep resistance from members of his own party, the prime minister, Sir Robert Peel decided to act. He had no alternative, and the Corn Laws were repealed by Parliament on 26 May 1846. Cheaper bread followed; it was a victory both for the 'free traders' and for the workers.

–

Cheaper bread was not the only result of the repeal of the Corn Laws. The issue split the Tory party. Peel's followers, known as 'Peelites', the free-trade advocates amongst whom was Gladstone, eventually joined with the Whigs to be reconstituted as the new Liberal party. The Tory party continued under the leadership of the 'protectionists' Lord Stanley and Disraeli.

Agricultural interests were also affected deeply in the long term. Many farms began the move from arable to sheep farming to maintain their income. Sheep farming required fewer workers and so rural poverty increased. Imports of cheap American wheat followed in the 1870s. More and more of the population moved from the countryside to the towns and cities looking for work.

47 The LAST frontier conflict with the USA

15 June 1846

There were many conflicts, even wars, between Britain and the United States of America well after the War of Independence in the 18th century. The longest running dispute was over the territory to the north of the Columbia river in the extreme north-west of the what is now indisputably the USA. Britain's last territorial claim in the USA was here in frontier America, in Oregon; it was settled by treaty in 1846.

Since the early part of the 19th century Oregon had been the centre of considerable diplomatic activity between the two countries. Canadian fur traders had settlements there and in 1818 an agreement was reached that the official border between Canada and the USA was to be the 49th parallel. Despite this, a joint occupation of Oregon was agreed for a period of ten years. Nine years later the occupation was extended for an indefinite period.

During this time Oregon was dominated by the British Hudson Bay Company at Fort Vancouver on the Columbia river. A few fur traders and missionaries moved into the territory in a slow trickle.

In the early 1840s immigration from the USA began to increase. Farmers looking for land came over the Rocky Mountains via the 'Oregon Trail'. At first the parties braving the hardships of the long journey from the Mississipi were only a handful, but within a few years settlers were pouring into Oregon in their hundreds.

The dangers of the trail have been immortalised in many a western story since, but they were very real. The trail itself was rocky, very ill-defined and criss-crossed by streams, rivers and mountains. The attacks on the wagon trains by Indians were matched by the rigours of disease and wild animals. Those who made it to Oregon, to settle down on their own farms, felt it was all worthwhile.

The few Canadians and Britons in the territory were gradually swamped by the American settlers. By 1843, the first real year of the Oregon Trail, there could be no doubt about Oregon becoming part of the USA.

American politicians were by this time proclaiming that it was 'America's "Manifest Destiny" to overspread the continent allotted by Providence for the free development of our yearly multiplying millions.' The northern border with Canada soon became an issue again. James Polk, on being elected President in 1844, declared that the USA's title to Oregon was 'clear and unquestionable'. Opinions in Britain were equally firm the other way but it was really only a matter of time.

Eventually Britain had to compromise and a treaty was signed on 15 June 1846 giving the USA all the territory south of the 49th parallel except for Vancouver Island. All British claims on land south of this line were at an end.

–

Two years later Oregon became a Territory within the United States. The Hudson Bay Company moved out to Vancouver Island and the American immigrants settled down to enjoy their land. In 1859 Oregon became a State of the United States of America.

48 The LAST of the Royal Navy's semaphore
31 December 1847

In the early 19th century the Royal Navy had a most ingenious method of rapid communications between its headquarters in

London and its coastal and port commanders around southern England. A series of semaphore stations, manned round the clock, connected the Admiralty in Whitehall with its main ports at Portsmouth and Plymouth. In the days when travelling (and therefore communication) times were normally measured in hours or even days, messages on naval business would be relayed quickly from station to station, complicated information travelling hundreds of miles in a matter of minutes. This system served the Navy well throughout most of the wars with France. It continued throughout the 1820s and 1830s and was eventually replaced by electric telegraph in 1847.

The first semaphore stations were positioned around the coast in 1795. An arrangement of balls and flags were hoisted to send limited messages on the weather and other coastal navigation matters. This system was further developed and streamlined and a line of relay stations from London to Portsmouth opened in 1796. Complicated signalling boards, mounted on masts above the stations, consisted of batteries of shutters which were operated by ropes from below. An observer with a telescope read the signal from the adjacent station. This was repeated by the signallers in his own station for onward transmission.

The lines were expanded a few years later to include Plymouth in Devon and Chatham in Kent.

A highly sophisticated code system was devised which could cope with all the requirements of the Royal Navy's orders and commands.

When Britannia ruled the waves, semaphore helped speed messages to the ports which could despatch ships to the farthest corners of the globe. From the moment a plan was devised in Whitehall, a ship could set sail from Plymouth within an hour with full orders to carry out a complicated diplomatic or Naval mission. A speeding frigate reaching Plymouth with urgent news from a distant ocean could have its information on an admiral's desk in London within minutes.

The system generally was a great success. It was obviously dependent on good visibility and operation at night was usually impossible. On a good day however the Royal Navy could send its time signal from the Admiralty's Whitehall headquarters to Plymouth and back again in under three minutes – an almost unbelievable achievement.

At the end of the Napoleonic wars the lines were closed but in 1822 the line to Portsmouth was re-opened with a fully modernised system. Construction of a new line to Plymouth was also started but this was incomplete when abandoned in 1830.

The semaphore service maintained a regular uniformed corps of signallers. Over the next two decades they developed a proud tradition of service and performance.

In 1837 Sir Charles Wheatstone patented an 'electric telegraph' which was soon adopted by the railways. In 1844, Samuel Morse in America set up the first public telegraph, between Washington and Baltimore. Its capabilities were astounding and left any mechanical semaphore way behind.

Back in England, the Royal Navy were not slow to catch up. On 13 September 1847 the crews at all the semaphore stations received their notices. On the very last day of the year they were paid off and the semaphore closed down.

Today some of the stations still exist, curious reminders of an intriguing and truly successful communications system absolutely right for its time.

49 Wellington's LAST command

1848

The Duke of Wellington was by far the most distinguished British soldier of his time. He served brilliantly in the Army as a general as well as an administrator. He had served in Parliament, first in the House of Commons and later in the House of Lords. He not only fought with great tenacity against his country's enemies, he also devoted his later political career to fighting against parliamentary reform every inch of the way.

His many battles were fought in India, in the Peninsular campaigns of 1809-1814 and, of course, at Waterloo in 1815. His last 'campaign' was against a very appropriate foe – the revolutionary reformist Chartists. In 1848, when as an old man he was the Army's commander-in-chief, he took personal charge of organising the defence of London from the possible onslaughts

of the Chartist Movement.

1848 was the 'year of revolutions'. Throughout Europe, royal houses and governments were being swept away. In Britain the Chartist Movement was on the march and its leaders were preaching open rebellion. In Glasgow, in March, Chartist riots had taken place and the cavalry had to be called out to control them.

The Chartists' main demands were for parliamentary reform: annual elections, votes for all men, secret ballots, equal sized electoral constituencies; for MP's salaries and the abolition of a property qualification. In 1839 and 1842 petitions with millions of signatures had been handed in to Parliament but had been rejected on both occasions. This time an even larger petition had been collected. The Chartist leader Fergus O'Connor led the new demonstration in London. A rally at Kennington was to be followed by a march on Parliament with a monster petition reputed to weigh 6 tons and contain over five million signatures.

Wellington had 170,000 special constables sworn in and various companies of troops standing by. He blocked off the entrances to all the bridges over the river Thames. O'Connor was warned by the police that any march on the Houses of Parliament was illegal and would be prevented. In the end he left his supporters at Kennington and the petition was handed in peacefully. The duke's organisation was not found to be wanting.

The petition actually contained only two million signatures but many were duplicates. The Duke of Wellington himself appeared to have signed thirty times! Parliament yet again rejected the Chartist demands and cracked down on the movement with great severity. Many of its leaders were later convicted of sedition and transported for life. It was the last great Chartist demonstration.

Despite the petition being rejected, all the aims of the Chartists, except annual elections, were eventually achieved.

The Duke of Wellington died in 1852. In his time he had led both the British Army and the British Government. No other modern Briton has done so. His country spared him no honour and gave him enormous wealth. He was by the standards of his day a remarkably able man. Disraeli described him as 'the greatest man of a great nation – a general who had fought fifteen pitched battles, captured 3,000 cannon from the enemy and never lost a single gun.' No 19th century general could want a better epitaph.

50 The LAST cockfighting

1849

In its heyday in the 17th and 18th centuries cockfighting was the most popular sport in the British Isles. It appealed to all classes of society from royalty downwards and one of its main attractions was as an excuse for betting. Two cocks would be placed in a ring, or 'cockpit'. Bets were placed and huge sums of money could change hands at the end of the fight. The last legal cockfight in Britain took place in 1849, after which the practice was outlawed.

The natural aggression of cocks towards each other has been used throughout history to enable the staging of fights to the death. Betting on the outcome of such fights – on which bird would die and which would live – was the major incentive for the development of the sport.

Specially bred fighting cocks were very valuable. Their owners often gave them as much care and attention as race horses might receive today. The assets essential to a fighting gamecock – strength and aggression – were developed by careful breeding. To their natural abilities was added the practice of artificially sharpening their claws and beaks and, in many cases, attaching lethal metal spurs to their legs.

In the cities gentlemen and common labourers alike would attend a fight and win or lose fortunes on the outcome. The cockpits were often inside specially constructed buildings. In the towns and villages, fairs would bring a crop of cockfights and many smaller outdoor cockpits were to be found all over the country, often surrounded by a fence, next to a public house. Some fights were arranged with more than two birds, the winner being the last of the several birds on its feet.

In 1849 the sport of cockfighting was outlawed. The legislation at the time provided for a £5 fine for any offender. This date can therefore be regarded with absolute certainty as the occasion of the last legal cockfight.

Cockfighting is still permitted in many parts of the world. To this day there is no doubt that secret fights are still staged illegally in various parts of Britain. The cruel side to the human character will ensure that the sport will continue for many more years.

51 The LAST British conquests in India

21 February 1849

The end of the Second Sikh War in 1849 marked the end of the armed British conquest of India. The last battle of that war, at Gujrat, took place on 21 February 1849. The British force, commanded by Lord Gough, defeated the Sikh Army decisively and the Punjab was immediately occupied to become part of British India.

Until this period the Punjab was a separate independent state. In the 1830s it was ruled by Ranjit Singh. His Sikh Army was highly developed and, apart from the British East India Company's sepoy armies, was the most modern and efficient in the sub-continent of India. On Ranjit Sing's death in 1839 the new Sikh rulers began to look outside their borders for employment for their troops. The first war of British against Sikh was in 1846. There followed an uneasy period where the Punjab was nominally free, with a boy maharaja on the throne guided by some British advisers.

The Second Sikh war began in 1848, after two British political officers had been murdered in Multan, in the south-west of the Punjab. Two inconclusive battles, one at Ramnagar and the other at Chillianwallah, left the two opposing armies manœuvring in heavy rains in January 1849.

The British losses at Chillianwallah had the public and politicians at home baying for Gough's blood. His replacement was sent to relieve him of his command. The eighty year old Duke of Wellington had persuaded the dying Sir Charles Napier, the hero and conqueror of Scinde province, to return to India with the memorable words, 'If you don't do, I must.'

Before Napier could reach the Punjab, however, the last battle of the war was fought and, to the relief of the British nation, won.

Gough had a force of 25,000 men and ninety-six guns. He and his army finally encountered the Sikhs, led by Sher Singh and his father Chattar Singh, who had an army of 60,000 men and fifty-nine artillery pieces, on grassy plains near Gujrat.

Both armies arrayed themselves in classic formations facing each other, guns and infantry at the centre, cavalry on the flanks. Gough's infantry advanced and the Sikh guns opened fire at a great distance. The British artillery replied and soon were tearing great holes in the Sikh ranks. The British infantry and cavalry again advanced and the Sikh lines broke. All their guns were captured and the entire Sikh Army, including their commanders, surrendered or were put to flight. The last remnants surrendered to British-led troops on 14 March near the North West Frontier. The Sikh resistance in the Punjab was over.

–

The tactics employed throughout the two Sikh wars were reminiscent of those used at Waterloo, and even earlier. Many of the British soldiers were actual veterans of those campaigns. Gujrat marked the end of the set piece battles on the the Indian sub-continent. It was also the last major battle in which the Sepoy troops took part. After the Mutiny in 1857, the East India Company was dismantled and the Indian Army was formed to replace the company's troops.

Sikh resistance was over, for the moment, and the Punjab was annexed by the British on 7 April. Although defeated in battle the Sikhs were never really conquered. Their soldiers have served honourably and with great distinction in the Indian Army ever since. Today the Punjab is still part of India, but the fiery spirit of the Sikh nation makes them as independent-minded as ever, presenting to the Indian Government a series of problems at least as difficult as those faced by the British Raj.

52 The LAST of the Navigation Acts
1 January 1850

Restrictive laws to prevent foreign shipping from competing on equal terms with British shipping existed as long ago as the 14th century. Various laws ensured that only British ships carried British cargoes to and from Britain. These laws were gradually reduced in effectiveness over the years and finally, at the start of

1850, they were rescinded in a positive move towards free trade.

Britannia in the 19th century really did rule the waves, but it had not always been so. Britain's merchant fleet had sometimes been small and frail. Various laws were passed to protect it and to encourage more shipbuilding. Since the time of Richard II a series of Navigation Acts had been passed by English and later by British Parliaments to favour British shipping at the expense of foreign ships. In the period of Cromwell's Commonwealth England's greatest rival was the Netherlands. Laws that were hostile to Dutch and Scandinavian shipping interests were passed to encourage trade with the British Colonies rather than with Europe.

By the end of the 17th century Britain was the greatest trading country in the world. It had near monopolistic links with the East, with Europe with the American colonies. By the 19th century these trading routes had expanded still further and it was generally recognised that British industry and commerce no longer needed the protection that these laws gave. In addition, it was thought, the competition from foreign shipping would provide a new stimulus to shake up some of the more complacent and inefficient shipowners in England and Scotland.

The British Colonies too were keen on the removal of the Navigation Laws as it would free their trade enabling it to be carried by more than just British ships.

America had similar laws to protect their shipping and, it was agreed, it would be in the best interests of all countries if the restrictions were lifted by both countries.

In the early part of the parliamentary session of 1849 the President of the Board of Trade, Labouchere, introduced the motion that would 'remove the restrictions which prevent the free carriage of goods by sea to and from the United Kingdom and the British Dominions abroad'.

The free traders did not have it all their own way. Protectionists still abounded in Parliament, among them Disraeli, but the bill was eventually passed and the Navigation Acts were duly abolished on 1 January 1850.

–

The free-trading British merchant navy maintained its world domination for many more decades. Although in some countries only lip service is paid to free trade, nothing quite so blatantly nationalistic as the British Navigation Acts exists today.

53 Turner's LAST painting

1850

Joseph Mallord William Turner is recognised as probably the greatest painter Britain has ever produced. He achieved fame and recognition early, lived an eccentric, independent life and produced his last major oil paintings in 1850.

Turner was only twenty-four years old when he became an Associate of the Royal Academy in 1799. His work, in both oils and watercolour, was given full and early recognition by the art world. He travelled extensively in Britain and on the continent, sketching and collecting details for his paintings. His work was mainly in a highly individual expressionistic style, full of light and colour giving an atmosphere that is still unique. His paintings of the sea and ships, in dramatic views, were breathtaking and greatly appreciated by the public.

He had amazing abilities to paint quickly and almost without plan. Turner had the unnerving, rather unfair habit of hanging his paintings at exhibitions in a semi-complete state. During the three or four days reserved for varnishing he would add the final details, often deliberately adding features and colours to upstage the work of notable painters hanging nearby.

His private life was secretive and he was notoriously unsociable. For ten years he lived with his mistress, Sarah Danby, and had two illegitimate children. He never married; the last years of his life were spent in semi-seclusion in a cottage in Chelsea. He hoarded his money with aggressive miserliness and became enormously wealthy.

His output was truly prodigious. He painted hundreds of oil pictures and many thousands of watercolours and sketches. His last four oils were painted in 1850 and exhibited at the Royal Academy in that year. They were all on the related theme of Dido and Aeneas. The last of these was *The Departure of the Fleet* which today hangs in the Tate Gallery in London.

On his death in December 1851 Turner was buried in St Paul's Cathedral. It was found that he had left his £140,000 fortune to establish a charity for 'decayed artists'. His collection of his own paintings, which included over a hundred oils – some of which he had bought back from the original purchasers – was left to the nation on the condition that it be accommodated in a suitable gallery within ten years.

The nation did not treat Turner's wishes very seriously. The public had to wait until 1908, for his paintings to be displayed at the Tate Gallery. Protracted litigation by distant relatives prevented forever his fortune from helping any 'decayed artists'.

54 The LAST of the window tax
24 July 1851

One of the more infamous taxes devised by the British Government was the window tax. It was first introduced in 1696 and lasted with varying degrees of strictness for over 150 years until the rationalisation of taxation in the middle of the 19th century.

Obviously a tax which was levied on house owners and depended on the number of windows in a building led to some strange architecture. Stopped up windows were common to avoid at least some of the taxes. Some buildings were designed and built with false window spaces to preserve the correct proportions. More important, for the poorer classes, smaller houses had so few window spaces that the health of its occupants suffered.

The tax reached its peak in the Napoleonic wars. The Government, ever on the look-out for ways of increasing revenue to pay for the wars, had increased window tax for a building with up to six windows to 8s a year. Owners of buildings with more than six windows had to pay proportionally more.

Window tax was finally abolished on 24 July 1851, income tax was already a major source of funds for the Government's coffers and it was an appropriate time to get rid of such an incongruous tax. Just a couple of months earlier the Great Exhibition had been opened in the Crystal Palace, specially constructed for the purpose in London's Hyde Park. The sheer acreage of its glass windows was a suitable monument to the new age of freedom in fenestration!

—

False windows, often painted to resemble the real thing, can still be seen in some 18th century buildings today – a strange legacy of a past taxation system.

55 The LAST duel

1852

It is difficult to say precisely when affairs of honour, or duels, actually became illegal in Britain. The last duel in England however, where the antagonists faced each other at dawn with pistols, was at Egham in Surrey in 1852. Two Frenchmen were involved in defending their honour, a Monsieur Barthélemy mortally wounding a Monsieur Cournet.

William the Conqueror introduced the Trial by Battle as part of the feudal system of justice. Two nobles, or their appointed champions, would fight it out, to the death if necessary, to settle a dispute – to the victor went the argument. It was generally supposed that God would intervene on the side of right and ensure both victory and justice at one literal stroke. Trial by Battle understandably fell into disuse but remained on the statute books for England until 1819.

By the 15th century duelling had become a cult. An argumentative gentleman, entitled to wear a sword, often felt obliged to use it on receipt of an insult however slight or unintended.

An act of Oliver Cromwell in 1654 forbade duelling; and Charles II, not many years later, also had to issue a proclamation against the practice.

By the 18th century society was beginning to stir against the futility of young men killing each other over pretended slights. Beau Nash, the famous society host at Bath, forbade not only tobacco in his rooms but swords as well. This did much to change society's view of what was acceptable behaviour.

The wearing of swords in public died with the 18th century but affairs of honour continued. Now it was with pistols, usually specially made for the purpose in matched pairs. Strict rules applied to the duels: seconds, surgeons and independent observers all played a part on the deserted fields and commons to see the ritual through.

If a fatality occurred the surviving duellist could be charged with manslaughter, but would usually manage to escape and live quietly for a few months until the fuss had died down.

By this time the idea of killing the opponent was often the least of the intentions. 'Honour satisfied' was the aim, with the protagonists firing into the ground or deliberately missing their targets, so long as the gentlemen did not flinch in the face of the flaring pistols.

Habits died hard however. 'Satisfaction' was regularly granted to participants in quarrels among army officers. Even dukes fought duels, even well-known ones. Possibly one of the most famous quarrels was the Duke of Wellington's, when prime minister, with Lord Winchilsea in 1829. The affair ended in Battersea Fields where neither of the duellists aimed at each other when discharging their pistols.

By the 1840s public opinion had thoroughly turned and the duel was no longer acceptable. The law against it began to be applied with more and more vigour, many duellists ending in prison for manslaughter.

One of the last publicly acknowledged duels in England was fought in July 1843 – predictably between two army officers. Lieutenant Alexander Munroe of the Horse Guards was killed by Colonel Fawcett of the 55th Regiment. The result of this killing was public outcry at such behaviour and the formation of an Anti-duelling Association. Fawcett fled the country but eventually returned to face trial and was convicted of manslaughter.

Pressure was brought to bear on the authorities. In the Army, duelling was not only forbidden but an Article of War – which had actually obliged officers to 'redeem their honour' in a duel – was repealed in 1844.

A few more duels did take place but now, conducted in great secrecy, they gave little cause for satisfaction. The last recorded death by duelling at Egham in 1852, Monsieur Cournet's, brought this extraordinary ritual to an end in the British Isles.

–

Duels of course continued abroad. Many an English gentlemen, in fact and in fiction, used the ferry to Boulogne to meet his opponent and look at him along the barrel of his pistol. In Britain however the affairs of honour were over.

56 The LAST of the press gang

1853

By the end of the 18th century the most common method for the Royal Navy to obtain the huge numbers of seamen that it required was by 'impressment'. During the Napoleonic wars the press gangs would roam the streets of Britain's seaports capturing and taking men forcibly into the Navy. Officially they were supposed to take only trained seamen, supposedly from the merchant service, but in practice any able-bodied male was liable to being hauled away for indefinite duty in the hard and dangerous world of the Royal Navy's warships.

The system lasted until the 1850s when the conditions of service for naval ratings were changed. In 1853 the Navy introduced a system for training and for fixed terms of service; the provision of crews for Her Majesty's ships became the responsibility of the Government rather than the local ports or the captains of the ships.

There were many volunteers in the Royal Navy but in time of war this method of manning was never enough. If the captain of a ship required more men to keep his ship properly run he organised a press gang when he reached port. In the busy naval ports this often led to rival press gangs, from different ships, fighting each other for the hapless impressed men.

There were few exceptions as to who might be taken. No training in naval duties was required and the newly conscripted men soon learned the ropes alongside the old hands on board. Those who could not learn did not last long.

As the numbers of men available for the ships became fewer, especially at the height of the wars with France, the responsibility for pressing was given over to a centrally organised Impress Service. Additionally, in 1795, the country was divided and each area was given the responsibility to find a certain quota of likely men. These were usually found in the prisons and the magistrates courts. As the life in the Navy was even more vicious than in the Army (the local militia, too had a quota to be filled) if there was any choice in the matter the Navy was left with the dregs.

In terms of human misery the system was a disaster; as a way of running a successful fighting navy the system, incredibly, seemed to work. Brutal times required brutal solutions and life in the Navy's ships had never been an easy one.

The Continuous Service Act was passed by Parliament in 1853. This provided for the recruitment of young men who were to be trained before they went to sea. A fixed term of service was defined. The numbers of older men who had experienced almost indefinite service, 'the Queen's hard bargains' originally from the prisons, died out. The crews now were generally younger, more respectable and certainly more humanely treated.

–

The tramp of the press gangs on the cobbled backstreets of the ports and seaside villages faded away. Conscription – along with all the paraphernalia of paperwork that bureaucracy could devise – returned to Britain only many years later, in 1916 during the First World War. Ironically, when it did, it was the Royal Navy and not the Army that was then considered the 'soft option'.

57 The LAST of the 'taxes on knowledge'

June 1855

The fight for the freedom of the British press was partly a battle against the taxes imposed on it. In addition to some draconian laws on libel and sedition, the newspaper proprietors in the 18th and 19th centuries had to contend with several different taxes. Most of them were intended to curtail circulation and thereby control criticism of the Government, rather than as *bona fide* methods of raising money. The availability of newspapers to the poorer classes was thus severely limited. High cover prices, equivalent in some cases to more that a day's wages, ensured that the open discussion of political writings was the preserve of the rich. Early trade unionism was severely restricted in its influence by the high tax on its journals.

The most notorious of these taxes, the newspaper stamp duty, was, after a long, hard campaign, abolished in 1855, opening the way to a rapid expansion of the national press.

The first newspaper tax was introduced in Britain in 1712 specifically to control the flow of information to the public. The Industrial Revolution brought a stimulation of intellectual discussion and a thirst for information. In the early part of the 19th century details on the war with France were eagerly sought after and provided by popular journalism.

All newspapers had to be licensed and each copy was printed with a small red stamp in its corner which signified that the publication was acceptable to the authorities and that the licence duty had been paid.

By the end of the Napoleonic wars this duty was 4d per copy sold. It was extended to include magazines which previously had been left untouched. In addition to this tax, any advertisements were also subject to a tax of 3s 6d and the paper itself was taxed at 3d for every pound weight. Each publishing enterprise was then also liable to 10% income tax. No newspapers could be legally produced and sold for under 7d. Despite this, in 1815 there were six daily newspapers in London alone with circulation figures ranging from several hundred to several thousand. The industry became highly developed in spite of the restrictions but only the wealthy could afford them. The practice of renting newspapers for a few hours was commonplace and many regular readers combined together to buy them.

Many legitimate proprietors were not shy in declaring their opposition to the taxation. The *Examiner*, a weekly periodical, carried a banner on its cover explaining its price, 'Paper and Print 3 1/2d; Taxes on Knowledge 3 1/2d; price 7d'.

Many different ways of avoiding the payment of the duty were devised. Many 'unstamped' periodicals sprang up, avoiding the duty. Being cheaper they became available to most of the population. Some unstamped papers achieved circulation figures of 30,000 or 40,000 copies, equalling and surpassing some of the legal stamped press. (The daily circulation of the famous 'Thunderer', *The Times*, was around 40,000 in 1850.)

The *Poor Man's Guardian* was a celebrated case. Established in 1831 by a Mr Hetherington to protest and uphold 'this grand bulwark of all our rights, this key to all our liberties, the freedom of the press', it boldly described itself on the front page as a 'Weekly newspaper for the People. Published contrary to law.'

Extraordinary measures were taken to prevent the authorities intervening. The newspaper had offices in the Strand in London which were continually watched by the police. Dummy parcels were despatched from the front door to occupy the police whilst the real copies were collected from the back. Hetherington himself often had to enter and leave the premises disguised as a Quaker. He spent several terms in prison but eventually won an important court case in 1834 which established that the law as it stood did not apply to his paper.

In 1836 the stamp duty was considerably reduced, from 4d to 1d. The Government realised that it was impossible to banish completely all illegal publications, so it was felt that a greatly reduced tax (with free postage thrown in) might encourage acceptance of the law.

The fight for the complete removal of the taxes went on. The Newspaper Stamp Abolition Committee was formed in 1849 by the Chartist Movement. Prominent campaigners of the day, Cobden, Bright and Collett among many others, formed an Association for the Repeal of the Taxes on Knowledge.

The last bastions began to crumble. In 1853 the advertisement tax was abolished. The redoubt itself fell in June 1855 when the stamp duty was repealed. Finally, the very last outpost, the iniquity of the duty on the actual paper used, was removed in 1861 by Gladstone after a last flurry of resistance from the House of Lords.

—

It had been a long fight but the result was cheap national newspapers. The first penny paper was the *Daily Telegraph*, formed in the year of the stamp duty abolition. The *Manchester Guardian*, the *Yorkshire Post* and the *Birmingham Post* soon followed. A fundamental right for the British people to cheap information was established.

58 The LAST Sheffield Plate

1855

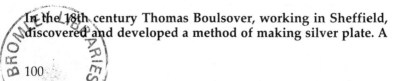

In the 18th century Thomas Boulsover, working in Sheffield, discovered and developed a method of making silver plate. A copper ingot, sandwiched between two ingots of silver, was heated and rolled flat. The resulting sheets were used in much the same way as solid silver to make high quality decorative silverware but at much cheaper prices. Sheffield Plate, as it came to be called, was manufactured in enormous quantities as a cheap alternative to silver until the middle of the 19th century when it was superseded by electroplate.

At first Sheffield Plate was used to imitate as closely as possible the solid silver articles it was replacing. This imitation often went as far as the silver marks themselves – the markings used were designed to look very similar to sterling silver hallmarks. Later the manufacturers of Sheffield Plate articles progressed and the designers began to come up with their own unique styles. In 1784 the silver manufacturers in Sheffield managed to get authority to register the marks they were using. Hundreds did so; the last one registered was in 1836. Also, any manufacturers within a hundred miles of Sheffield had to register their marks at the Sheffield Silver Assay Office. This included, much to their chagrin, all of Birmingham's Sheffield Plate factories.

In 1840 Birmingham had their revenge. The Elkington Company in Birmingham invented and patented a process for electroplating silver onto copper. This process was much cheaper than Sheffield Plate and could be applied to otherwise completely finished items, usually mass-produced. This new EPNS, electroplated nickel silver, very rapidly replaced Sheffield Plate. By 1855 the Sheffield Plate industry was virtually dead, limited for a few further years to the manufacture of buttons, belt buckles and a few coach lamps.

–

Today Sheffield Plate is avidly sought after by collectors. Though originally a substitute for the 'real thing', it has a high intrinsic value; most items were made by highly skilled craftsmen. Forgeries abound – a sure sign of collectability. Ironically, electroplated silverware, purporting to be Sheffield Plate, is the commonest type of fake.

59 The LAST of the Vauxhall Gardens

1855

Vauxhall Gardens in south London were once the exciting playgrounds for Londoners of all classes. They were at their peak in the early 19th century, the Regency period, when thousands of London's 'society' spent their summer evenings in the gardens, strolling and eating, watching the dancing and singing. The popularity of the pleasure gardens faded in the 1830s and 1840s and in 1855 the Gardens were closed forever, the land being sold for building.

Vauxhall Gardens were on the site of the manor of Fauxe Hall, on the south bank of the river Thames. Samuel Pepys records visiting the 'Spring Gardens', as they were first known, 'at Fox Hall' although it was not until the early part of the 18th century that they became really popular, the owner putting on open air entertainment *'ridotto al fresco'*. Musical evenings with dancing girls, fireworks and circus acts drew the crowds.

Dr Johnson was a frequent visitor, commenting 'it is peculiarly adapted to the taste of the English nation; there being a mixture of curious show, gay exhibition, music, vocal and instrumental, not too refined for the general ear, for all of which only a shilling is paid; and, though last not least, good eating and drinking for those who choose to purchase that regale'.

Visitors were free to walk along eleven acres of winding paths, past follies and colonnaded ruins, fountains and statues, lit by thousands of lamps. Balloon ascents and even some attempted parachute jumps were performed. The numerous bandstands, coffee rooms and eating places were highly popular. The more secretive parts of the gardens were widely acknowledged as the use for rendezvous for lovers.

The gardens, however, did not last. As they became more popular and the entrance fee was reduced, the type of visitor changed. Visits from royalty became fewer and the Duke of Wellington, once a common stroller at Vauxhall, now shunned the place. The place grew more seedy and, it was said, the very trees and shrubs looked worn out.

Every year, Londoners were told, was going to be positively

the last year. But they lasted until the autumn of 1855 when the last paying visitors were ushered from the gates.

Nearby Battersea Fields were bought by the Government. They were landscaped and planted and opened to the public in 1858 to become one of London's most popular parks. In 1859 the public were allowed into Vauxhall Gardens for the last time – for the auction of effects. 274 lots: paintings, lamps, statues, fountains and furniture were all disposed of at knock-down prices. Buildings were soon built on the Gardens. Times had changed and more demure, austere, outdoor pursuits were the order of day.

60 The LAST of the Crimean War

25 November 1855

The war that was fought in the coastal regions of the far-off Black Sea, the Crimean War, was a struggle against Russian aggression by Turkey. In this she was assisted by France and Britain. The four best remembered battles, at the Alma River, at the siege of Sebastapol, the cavalry charges at Balaclava and bravery at Inkerman, were not the only memorable ones. In fact the very last battle of the war was one that was lost by the Allies, at Kars in Armenia where a British officer in command of Turkish troops eventually surrendered to the Russians in November 1855.

By the middle of 1854 the temporary relief gained by the Turks in Anatolia by the French and British presence in the Crimea had gone. The Russians were determined to capture the important Turkish Armenian frontier town of Kars. Lieutenant Colonel Fenwick Williams with a small group of staff officers was ordered to Kars, arriving in September to find it under siege. The Turkish troops, a garrison of 28,000, were in dire need of every conceivable item of supplies from ammunition to food, clothing and back-pay. By the spring of the following year, Williams, now a lieutenant general, was leading the Turkish soldiers against assaults from the surrounding Russian Army. The defenders held on gallantly, the Turkish troops performing exceptionally well, and the attack was repelled.

Food for the besieged garrison however was running out fast; the Russians made a feint withdrawal and then attacked with renewed vigour on 29 September in three columns with supporting artillery.

The defenders fought hard and bravely and at the end of this ferocious battle Williams and his Turkish soldiers were temporarily victorious. 5,000 Russian bodies lay on the plains before Kars. Another 7,000 dead and wounded were carried away by the Russians as they fell back exhausted. The Turkish losses were less than a thousand.

Despite this temporary defeat for the Russians time was definitely on their side. They did not withdraw far and their commander, Mouravieff, ensured that their encampments circling the fortress of Kars were made even more permanent.

The occupants of Kars were starving to death. No food could be got in and no-one could get out. The soldiers resorted to eating their horses. Even the grass that they could get to under the snow was dug up for possible sustenance. Cholera struck with vicious certainty and, in a period of two weeks in early October, killed over a thousand men. Hopes of a relief column under the Turkish commander Selim Pasha faded. The garrison under General Williams was on its own.

Williams finally determined on an honourable surrender. With an aide he made his way through enemy lines to the Russian camp and there he met with Mouravieff face to face. Williams laid out his terms, saying to the astonished Russian that if not granted 'every gun shall be burst, every standard burnt, every trophy destroyed and you may work your will on a famished crowd.'

Honourable terms were agreed on 25 November 1855. The Turkish soldiers were allowed to return to their homes and the British and Turkish officers were allowed to keep their swords as they were taken – with great courtesy – into custody in Russia as prisoners-of-war.

The Russians took all of Turkish Armenia and so ended the campaigning.

–

Despite the Turkish and Allied loss of Kars, Russia's will was broken after their forced abandonment of Sebastapol earlier in the year. Perhaps because of the Russian victory at Kars the new Czar

The Russians are repelled from their
attack on Kars in Armenia. The town
was defended bravely by Turkish
soldiers, but reports of the action as a
defeat for the Russians were
premature. Within a month General
Williams, commanding the Allies'
forces, surrendered after what was to
be the the last battle of the Crimean
War.

was able to make a very necessary peace without too much loss of face. The war ended early in 1856 after the Treaty of Paris, with the Russian Bear and the Black Sea neutralised and the Turkish Empire propped up to survive for a few more decades.

61 The LAST prison hulks

1857

Prison hulks were the hulls of de-commissioned Royal Navy ships-of-the-line. They were first used as temporary prisons in 1776. Positioned on the downstream banks of the river Thames and other major estuaries, each held hundreds of prisoners. In the close dark spaces of the old rotting ships' hulls, the occupants were confined in conditions of great depravity. Discipline was difficult to enforce by the authorities and on board disease and vice of every kind could be found. As the more formal land-based jail building programme got under way, the need for the hulks diminished. Their use was finally discontinued in 1857.

The use of hulks was, at first, a temporary measure. But like so many temporary measures it became permanent out of necessity. They were originally intended to hold convicts before they were transported. Transportation to the American colonies had to be stopped during the War of Independence with America and when the war was over a new destination had to be found. Those convicts waiting for their sentence were held on board the hulks to await events. Ten years later some were still waiting and life on the hulks had become a way of life.

Gradually over the years incarceration in the hulks became the sentence in itself. The convenience and cheapness of a floating prison, however unsavoury the conditions on board, was too hard to resist for any Government needing to save money.

Usually the sentences included hard labour; gangs of prisoners were marched ashore daily to carry out back-breaking labour in some public works project nearby.

The sad old decaying warships, their rigging and masts removed, were a grim sight on the river banks of the major ports of England. The convict gangs who were imprisoned on board every night were a stark reminder to the passer-by of the inadequacies of the jail system.

By 1842 the prison population of the hulks had peaked at over 3,000. The main hulks of *Justitia*, *Leviathan*, *Stirling Castle*, *Warrior* and *York* each had more than 500 prisoners aboard.

But reformers were active. A vast prison building programme was in hand and even by 1840 the need for the hulks was declining. The last was abandoned by the prison service in 1857 and broken up for scrap.

−

'Hulks' or at least their equivalent have been used since then. In the 1970s, in Belfast Lough in Northern Ireland, internment prisoners were held temporarily on various ships until more permanent prisons ashore could be found for them.

62 The LAST official discrimination of Jews

1858

At the beginning of the 19th century Jews in Britain had very few rights. But as the prejudices against Catholics, Irish immigrants and foreigners gave way to reason, so practising Jews were gradually admitted to most parts of society as respectable, useful Britons. The last bastion of prejudice against Jewry was in the Houses of Parliament, where Jews were eventually allowed to become members in 1858. The last Jew actually to be forcibly prevented from taking his rightfully elected seat in the House of Commons was Alderman Salomons, elected member for Greenwich in London, in 1851.

The Jewish race was treated with contempt by many British Christians during the 19th century. In addition to the religious overtones of this mistrust, Jews were often involved in banking and money-lending; resentment of their often spectacular successes in these fields contributed to the hatred which they received.

Official, legal prejudice remained pervasive. Several Jews had been elected to high office and special Acts of Parliament had to be

107

passed to enable them to hold these positions. This had happened to Salomons in 1835 when he was elected to be Sheriff of London. In 1846 Jews were eventually permitted to hold elected municipal office.

Before Salomons had been elected to Parliament Baron Rothschild had made an attempt. He had been returned for the City of London in 1850 but his request to swear his oath of allegiance, before entering Parliament, on the Old Testament instead of the New Testament was refused.

The next year legislation was introduced to enable Jews to take their oath without the Christian references. While this legislation was being debated Alderman Salomons was elected as Member of Parliament for Greenwich. Before he took his seat he too objected to having to swear on the New Testament and use the words 'on the true faith of a Christian'. He boldly refused to leave the chamber and actually took part in the debates and the voting on whether he should be allowed to take his seat. The voting went against him and he was eventually led away by the Sergeant-at-Arms. Petitions from his constituents followed but nothing was done as the legislation to permit Jews had been thrown out by the House of Lords.

In the meantime action in the Court of Exchequer had been brought against Salomons, for sitting and voting in Parliament without taking the oath – a criminal offence. He was fined £500.

Many more attempts were made in the House of Commons, led by Lord John Russell, to amend and reform the law. Each was blocked by the House of Lords. Eventually the House of Commons in 1858, by a resolution of its own, allowed Jews to be admitted.

Finally in 1860 an Act was passed to allow Jews to omit the Christian oath on taking office.

–

Disraeli, a well known and famous parliamentarian by this time, although he was from Jewish stock, was not a practising Jew; so he had not been debarred for the Commons. In today's political world, although legal prejudices still exist against other groups in society, Jews in the British Parliament now pass unnoticed on their way to hold high office.

63 The LAST county to create its police force
1862

Many counties in England and Wales had their own police forces, under local government control, by the end of the 1840s. There were however some which were still operating a system of local part-time parish constables. An Act of Parliament in 1856 forced all counties and boroughs, which had not already done so, to form their own police force. In order to obtain a grant of money from central government they had to submit to central inspections. The last county to achieve a fully operational police force was Rutlandshire in 1862.

The County and Borough Police Act introduced by Palmerston when he was Home Secretary was much opposed by mayors and borough corporations from all over the country who thought the whole idea 'centralised and tyrannical'. Nevertheless the Act forced all boroughs and counties to establish fully manned and disciplined forces. Standards of discipline and the numbers of constables per head of population were set down.

Rutlandshire had first ventured into the world of running its own police in 1848 when it set up a force consisting of one chief constable and just one constable to look after the entire – admittedly tiny – county of 12,000 people.

The complete legislation, as originally planned in 1854, would have forced small counties such as Rutland to combine with others. That particular clause of the Bill, however, did not appear when the Act was eventually passed in 1856, so Rutlandshire remained on her own. It took a further six years before the county was finally satisfactorily inspected and judged as possessing an efficient force.

–

The Rutlandshire police force lasted some ninety years until 1951 when it was combined, in name as well as in fact, with the neighbouring Leicestershire force. In 1974, following the reorganisation of local government boundaries, Rutlandshire itself, Britain's smallest county, was absorbed into Leicestershire and the name disappeared.

64 The LAST square pianos

1863

An important phase in the history of the piano was the development of the square or 'table' piano. This had a light single-action mechanism with which to hit the strings and had the shape of a long rectangular table. Square pianos were usually made entirely of wood with no metal bracing – their durability was never a strong point. They required less space than a grand piano, however, so they were popular in the British home until replaced by the upright piano around the middle of the 19th century. Although they were developed further in America, the last square piano made in England was constructed in 1863.

The earliest pianos, in size and shape, were based on the harpsichord. The hitting action, which replaced the plucking action of the harpsichord, produced new sounds and possibilities which gradually became recognised by the composers of the time. Mozart in particular embraced the new 'pianoforte', as it became universally known, and developed a style of composition which left the harpsichord well behind.

The design of the first square pianos resembled a large box, resting on a special stand, with the keyboard on the long side, rather than at the end as with a grand piano. Later the 'square' had its own legs, usually six – four along the front and two at the back. The full range of notes on a square piano was five octaves and a half compared to the seven found on most pianos today. They were relatively simple and cheap to make and they took up far less space than the grand pianos. They therefore had a special place in the parlours of the time where large volume and range were not needed.

Square pianos became very popular in Britain and were made by the English manufacturers such as Broadwood in very large numbers. Most piano manufacturers made both grand and square pianos – and later all three types, when the upright gained in popularity.

It was around 1810 that the very first upright pianos were made. They took up even less space than a square – although at first the strings started at keyboard level so they needed tall-ceilinged rooms. Gradually the uprights developed into the compact, cheap and very reliable instruments we know today. Their metal frames ensured good tuning and reliability. They were far more suitable for factory mass production and inevitably they overtook the square piano in numbers sold.

When manufacture of the square piano in England ceased, it continued for a while in the USA. The designs grew in size and strength. Iron frames were used to increase their sound and range. Even Steinway was making some remarkably successful square pianos as late as the 1880s. But for piano design the future was now set – the grands would dominate the concert halls and the uprights fill every front room. Today the surviving square pianos are a delightful throwback, bringing reminders of a more docile, gentle musical era.

65 The LAST of the 'wooden walls'

23 November 1863

In 1861 the *Warrior*, the first British warship to be built entirely of iron, was launched. All other warships – until then built of wood – were immediately made obsolescent. Old methods and ideas die hard and because it took several years to build a ship-of-the-line, for a few years wooden ships were still brought into service. The last all-wooden, first rate three-decker to be commissioned into the Royal Navy was the *Victoria*. It was almost identical to the ships that Britain's sailors had been sailing in for the previous 200 years.

Contrary to some accounts which indicate that the Royal Navy was over-cautious and highly resistant to new ideas, the middle of the 19th century was a period of exciting innovations and great change. In the 1850s the ships-of-the-line were sail-driven and made entirely from wood; they fired solid cannon balls through holes in the hull from muzzle-loading guns. By the 1880s the battle fleet consisted of steam-powered, iron-armoured ships firing explosive shells from turreted breech-loaders. For such a transition to have taken place, in the largest navy in the world, in time of

111

peace, was a considerable achievement.

The transition period lasted several years. Many battleships that were started as wooden sailing ships were converted to ironclads and steam power before launching. Several others were deliberately made of wood to use up the vast supplies of timber in the dockyards and then clad in iron armourplate.

The response to invention and new ideas, of course, came in fits and starts. Thus it was that *The Times* of London saw fit to criticise the efficacy of the obsolete *Victoria* which had had her keel laid in 1859. A week before she sailed on her first commission as flagship to the Mediterranean fleet the newspaper wrote: 'In time of war, the Admiral on board *Victoria* would have to decide between going into port or going to the bottom!'

Nevertheless she did sail, all magnificent 250 wooden feet and 3,000 tons of her, with a crew of 680 officers and ratings. Without any anomalies it could have pulled alongside any ship-of-the-line from the Napoleonic wars and not have been out of place. At 3 o'clock in the afternoon of 23 November 1864, the *Victoria* sailed from Spithead for Malta and, with her, the 'wooden walls of England' sailed into history.

—

The *Victoria* was the first of several Royal Navy ships to be named after Queen Victoria. She never saw action, which is just as well, as *The Times* was probably correct in its observation about her possible usefulness. She was sold for scrap in 1893.

66 The LAST 'handling' in football

1866

Football, as an organised game, began in the English public schools in the early years of the 19th century. It was very quickly adopted by northern working class clubs, most notably in the Sheffield and Nottingham areas. The rules of the game, played by different teams, varied widely. Each club had its own set of rules; whenever different teams met an agreement had to be reached before kick-off on which rules were to be used. 'Handling' of the ball was last permitted in 1863.

The early rules of Football, the so-called 'Cambridge Rules' of 1848, now seem not very different to those of Rugby. In particular, handling the ball was permitted, usually to enable the player to catch the ball and then either kick it immediately or make a 'mark', as in rugby, and be allowed a free kick. This was called the 'fair catch'. The player had to catch the ball cleanly and was not allowed to run with it or throw it, these distinctions being the main differences between football and Rugby.

The rules as they are known today finally came together in the mid-1860s shortly after the formation of the Football Association in 1863. Initially the FA consisted of eleven clubs, mainly southern English amateur sides. The long awaited big clash between the Football Association and the northern clubs came on 31 March 1866 with a game between Sheffield and London. It was at this time that the fair catch was abolished and the handling of the ball by the players, apart from the goalkeeper, banned.

Sheffield Football Club joined the Football Association a year later.

–

The rules have changed gradually ever since. In 1870, the last important variation between different clubs was done away with – universal agreement being reached that the regular number of players per team would be eleven.

67 The LAST Whigs

28 June 1866

The Whigs, who made up the political party which was in power for much of the 18th century, first came together in the last decades of the 17th century. They were in favour of restricting the Monarch's powers and increasing those of Parliament. The 19th century was to see their demise when they joined with some of the old Tory party to form the Liberals. Lord John Russell was the last Whig Prime Minister.

At the beginning of the 19th century party politics were sometimes difficult to disentangle, opponents one year becoming allies the next. The Whig Lord Melbourne, Queen Victoria's

Lord John Russell was a major
political figure of the 19th century
and the Great Reform Act of 1832
was perhaps his greatest
achievement. He resigned the
premiership in 1866 after his failure
to obtain parliamentary approval for
his second Reform Bill. When
Gladstone and his supporters
returned to power soon after, along
with the ex-Tory 'Peelites', they had
become known as Liberals. Russell
was the last Whig prime minister.

favourite prime minister in the late 1830s, had served quite happily a few years earlier under the arch-Tory, the Duke of Wellington. Without strong 'party machines' there was room for much flexibility amongst politicians. This applied to appointments as much as to party allegiance. For instance, acknowledged leaders of the parties were one thing but prime ministers were chosen by the sovereign. Thus in 1846, with Lord John Russell as the Whig Prime Minister, Palmerston was Foreign Secretary; fifteen years later the roles were reversed – Palmerston was Prime Minister with Russell as his Foreign Secretary.

Also, in the 1840s, a genuine new political party was in the making. The followers of Sir Robert Peel, known as 'Peelites', were loosening their ties with the remainder of the old Tory party, mainly over the issue of free trade and the repeal of the Corn Laws. Gladstone was one of the Peelites. Palmerston had resisted Parliamentary reform for thirty years. He was one of the last true Whigs and was Prime Minister on his death in 1865. When Palmerston left office and this world with the reassuring words, 'Die, my dear doctor? That's the last thing I shall do!', Russell succeeded to the premiership and to the leadership of the declining Whigs.

Russell, the third son of the Duke of Bedford, had been known by his courtesy title of Lord John Russell in the House of Commons. He had done sterling service thirty years earlier, steering the Great Reform Act through the Commons. In 1861 he was created an earl in his own right and elevated to the House of Lords.

There was a great public clamour for Parliamentary reform, mainly for the extension of the franchise to include the populous artisan classes in the big cities. On Palmerston's death the way was clear: Russell set to with relish.

Despite Disraeli's contention that 'England does not love coalitions' this was the final phase of the coalescing of the constituent parts of the Liberal party. The Peelites had found much in common with the Whigs and were part of Russell's administration. Gladstone, an ex-Peelite and now a confirmed 'Liberal', was leader in the House of Commons.

But Russell soon came unstuck with his Reform Bill. Moderate as it was, it could not find a majority in favour. Russell resigned in June 1866 and the last of the Whig prime ministers retired from active politics; he died in 1878.

–

The Tories under Lord Derby took over on 28 June. Disraeli, the Tory leader in the House of Commons, urged his own party to bring in the reforms 'to dish the Whigs'. So it was, ironically, the Tory Government that finally brought in the Reform Act of 1867 to extend the vote to a large proportion of the new working class. Thus, although Disraeli smoothly did dish the Whigs, retribution was swift. Lord Derby soon resigned and Disraeli, who then became Prime Minister, called a general election. The Liberals, now including the Radicals led by John Bright, finally came together and with Gladstone at their head were swept into office on the newly extended franchise.

68 The LAST of the East India Company

1 April 1867

The British East India Company was established in 1600 and built a huge commercial trading empire in the East. Its power was real and extensive; its influence prodigious. For most of its existence it was free from all interference from government and it took unto itself powers and duties synonymous with the mightiest of colonial powers. The Company's end finally came in the latter part of the 19th century.

Although it traded throughout the Far East, India was the Company's jewel in the crown – in more ways than one. The East India Company provided a vast and extensive administrative, military and civil empire as well as a trading framework. It had its own civil service, its own armies and of course its own traders. At the peak of its power it ruled over one-fifth of the world's population. In India it was known as 'John Company'.

The Company was not always scrupulous in all its dealings and such independence and power was not fully approved by the Government which was overseeing an expanding British Empire. At the end of the 18th century an Act of Parliament to some extent restricted and controlled the activities of the Company. Its twenty-four directors (elected by the shareholders) did control the day-to-day administration and of course the strictly commercial and trading activities. There was, however, another system of control – a secret inner committee of three directors who were in direct contact with the Government. It was they who controlled all political matters.

In 1834 the Company lost its monopoly of the far eastern and China trade, becoming more and more an administrative body, having fewer and fewer direct commercial functions.

Despite the trauma of the Indian Mutiny in 1857, which was certainly instrumental in motivating the Government to put an end to the Company's independence, the final chapter was yet to come.

After the Mutiny, the easy-going 18th century ways were gone for ever. The British Government stepped in and swept aside the Company. On 2 August 1858 all the powers that the Company had held were transferred to the Crown. British control in India, although arguably by today's standards flawed in principle, was to expand and develop into one of the finest examples of colonial Government ever seen.

But the British East India Company lingered on. Its smaller outposts were still spread throughout the Far East.

On 1 April 1867 the Straits Settlements, made up of Penang, Singapore and Malacca, were handed over by East India Company officials to the British authorities to become a Crown Colony. They were the Company's last possessions. Its business was over.

–

A few years later, in 1874, the East India Company was wound up and thereafter ceased to exist. The greatest, perhaps the most powerful 'multi-national' company ever, faded away almost unnoticed.

69 The LAST transportation

10 January 1868

The transportation of convicts to the wilder, more distant outposts of the world was first introduced by the British authorities in the early 1600s, primarily to the colonies of the New World. After the American War of Independence, distant Australia was used

instead. This eventually ceased after growing public protest in the 1860s.

In the 17th century, Virginia colonists were only too happy to buy the rights to convict labour so that they could run their plantations cheaply. But the use of this convenient dumping ground for criminals ended in the 1770s after American independence. The British Government was forced to find a new destination for its convicts. For strategic reasons, and after Africa had been ruled out on health grounds, the newly discovered continent of Australia was chosen.

In 1787 the first fleet of convicts and soldiers set sail from England to found the penal colony at Botany Bay in New South Wales. Thus the Australian colonies were born.

The treatment of criminals was a brutal, callous business in the 18th century. Transportation was considered a very useful solution to a tricky problem: it removed the 'criminal classes' from the homeland and put them to useful work and it punished them too. The convicts – men, women and children – were removed far from the home country in which they had committed their original offence – often the trivial theft of a few loaves of bread.

In a form of semi-slavery, they lived out their vicious and cruel sentences in a bleak, savage and hostile territory. At the end of their terms of punishment they were usually granted their 'ticket-of-leave' which forced them, under a continuing strict discipline, to live out the rest of their lives in Australia. Very few were permitted to return to Britain again.

As more and more free emigrants settled in Australia and as the iniquities of the system of bonded labour became widely known – in Britain as well as in Australia – pressure for the abolition of transportation grew.

The last remaining penal colony in the antipodes was Western Australia. It was almost wholly supported by the convict system and needed a thousand new convicts a year just to keep going. Most of the rest of Australia, the burgeoning eastern colonies which had already rejected convict labour, was adamant that transportation must stop. Finally, in 1865, Palmerston's Government in Britain agreed that the system would end.

In 1867 the last group of convicts to be transported set sail from Britain. Among the 451 prisoners were some sixty Fenian agitators from Ireland. They arrived at Fremantle in Western Australia on

10 January 1868 to begin their peculiarly harsh sentences.

In the short term the end of transportation was disastrous for Western Australia. But those colonies which put their reliance on bonded labour firmly behind them soon developed and grew. Britain. has much to be proud of in its colonial past, but its shiploads of convicts to Australia, numbering 160,000 persons in all spread over eighty years, must surely be one of the most questionable legacies ever bequeathed on one country by another.

70 The LAST public hanging
26 May 1868

The spectacle of the public execution of a convicted criminal was an awful sight but a common one in all parts of Britain for many centuries. The last such occasion was in 1868, outside Newgate Prison in London. Michael Barrett was a Fenian, an Irish patriot, who in trying to free two of his compatriots from Clerkenwell prison had planted a bomb outside the prison walls. When it exploded it killed four passers-by and wounded many others. Barrett went to his death, in public, knowing that he would be the last to do so – legislation for all future executions to be carried out inside prison walls had already passed through Parliament but was not due to receive royal assent until three days later.

The campaign for the reform of the law on all aspects of capital punishment had started many years earlier. At the turn of the 19th century there were over 150 crimes which attracted the death penalty. These ranged from the minor offences of robbery of goods worth more than 5s, sheep stealing and picking pockets to murder and high treason. Boys of less than ten years of age were hanged, in front of huge jeering crowds, for stealing trivial amounts of food needed to keep them alive. By the middle of the century only four capital offences remained but public hangings were drawing huge crowds. Apart from the moralistic condemnation of this public spectacle, the problems of maintaining law and order at these events was enormous. Thousands of people of all classes, from all

119

sections of society, would pack themselves in front of the prison, as close as possible to the temporary scaffold.

It was said that on an execution morning one saw faces that were never seen save round a gallows or a great fire. The crowds usually started to gather many hours before the event. The heaving masses of people fell easy prey to pick pockets and many other thieves and criminals. Riots often occurred and it was quite usual for members of the crowd to be crushed to death.

At the set time the criminals were led out from the prison, up onto the scaffold and, to yells of excitement and howls of execration from the crowd, dropped to their death.

William Ewart, a member of Parliament and an active abolitionist, was responsible for persuading Parliament to set up a select committee on capital punishment. One of the outcomes of this investigation was the measure, introduced by Hibbert, which in 1868 removed probably the most hideous aspect of capital punishment, the huge crowds who watched the hangings for entertainment.

On Tuesday 26 May 1868, however, it was Michael Barrett's turn – the new law being just too late to save him from public humiliation. He was twenty-seven years old and, although there had been several appeals against his conviction (he claimed he had been in Glasgow at the time of the crime), his sentence was upheld. He had no known relatives or friends present to see him die.

At 8am he was brought out of the side door of Newgate to mount the black gallows which had been dragged into position a few hours earlier. The crowd of nearly 40,000, the most part of which had been waiting all night, immediately went quiet. Barrett, wearing a short red jacket and grey striped trousers quietly submitted to his hands and legs being tied and went to his death with a serene dignity that put the crowd to shame. His body was cut down an hour later and the crowd was, with great difficulty, dispersed by the police.

The Times recorded this gruesome last occasion and the next day pontificated: 'London yesterday witnessed the last of those hideous spectacles familiar enough to the hard eyes of our predecessors but more and more repulsive to the taste of these days. We have only to think of the horror with which we all now instinctively regard the barbarous punishments inflicted lately down in our history and we may conceive what posterity will think of capital executions before a motley crowd of vulgar and often brutal spectators.'

—

Few people at the time utterly condemned capital punishment itself. Those who had hoped that the new Act against public execution would herald the abolition of the death penalty were to be disappointed. It took nearly another hundred years before the last person was executed in Britain. Notorious Newgate however was pulled down in 1903, to be replaced by the Central Criminal Court, the Old Bailey. In 1963 capital punishment was eventually abolished throughout Britain.

71 The LAST Dickens novel

June 1870

Charles Dickens, possibly Britain's greatest novelist, was a flamboyant man who loved the public admiration that he received in his own lifetime. In the last years of his life he became dedicated to giving public readings of his own books. With failing health, in 1869 he began to write his last book, *The Mystery of Edwin Drood*. Although publication in monthly parts had already begun, the book was unfinished when Dickens died in June 1870.

For his huge breadth of social vision Dickens was unrivalled in the 19th century. Full of comedy, romance and adventure, his stories were taken to the nation's heart. Eventually, translated into many languages, the world too came to know and love them. He was a campaigning writer; his subjects were always causes which the burgeoning middle classes wanted to know about. The public identified with his stories, and his books had a considerable influence on the social reforms of the time.

As well as being a superbly gifted writer he was an extremely able actor himself and he loved giving readings of his own work to large public audiences. The audiences loved him for it. His gruesomely realistic readings of Sikes murdering Nancy from his *Oliver Twist* had the ladies swooning with fright. On tours throughout Britain and the USA his adherents flocked in their thousands, devotedly queuing for tickets to his performances. Financially these readings provided him with an important part of his income – his tour of America made him a clear profit of £20,000.

Still committed to a punishing schedule of public readings in Britain, and despite failing health, Dickens began *The Mystery of Edwin Drood* in 1869 after a gap of four years after his previous novel. He received £7,500 for the copyright, with a half share of the profits. The story is one of murder and mystery, and has caused much discussion and controversy ever since it was published. Its unfinished nature adds to its own mystery; whether Drood is dead or alive remains unsolved as no completed plot was found.

Dickens gave his last reading in March 1870 in London just as the book's publication began in the usual monthly parts. It was received with acclaim and its sales exceeded those of all his other books. On 8 June he was busily writing, trying to add to the twenty-three chapters so far completed. He collapsed with a stroke that evening; the following day he was dead.

–

Opinions on *The Mystery of Edwin Drood* at the time were varied. Some thought it was 'a last laboured effort, the melancholy work of a worn out brain'. Others thought it his masterpiece. It was certainly the last of what is arguably the most famous list of fiction in the English language.

72 The LAST of the Academic Religious Tests

June 1871

The main centres of learning in England until the 19th century were at the universities of Oxford and Cambridge, London and Durham. At all of these except London (the most junior of the establishments) religious tests were applied to all entrants to ensure that only adherents of the Church of England could attain high honours and fill the important posts. The last year when the tests were applied was in 1871. At this time, the year in which Newnham, the first women's college at Cambridge was founded, Parliament altered the law to allow persons of any religious belief to hold office, take up posts and to qualify for masters degrees, thus ending the last academic restrictive religious practice in Britain.

The admission of dissenters to Oxford and Cambridge Colleges was a long-running sore in the academic and political life of England. Equality of opportunity in education – not then a universally held belief anyway – was confined to wealthy gentlefolk with the right connections who held the belief that the Church of England was the only acceptable religious faith.

Dissenters, that is those of the protestant religion who were not in the Church of England, were excluded from taking up the posts of influence in the Universities – the Fellowships. Also, unless he indicated his assent to the '39 articles' of faith, even a graduate could not qualify for a Master's degree. (which among other things entitled him to vote for that peculiar academic tributary of democracy, the University member of Parliament, an institution that survived until 1949).

In Gladstone's Government of 1868 dissenters were particularly strong. The abolition of the University Tests had become a particular reform with which the Liberal party was anxious to grapple.

In June 1871 the Universities Test Act became law. Now, only for studies and Fellowships in divinity would any form of test be applied. The road to religious academic freedom was opened.

–

Although moves to disestablish the Church of England were perhaps at their peak during this period, they never succeeded. The Anglican church still has an official, legal position in the the United Kingdom.

73 The LAST purchase of Army commissions

1 November 1872

One of the great features of the British Army in Victorian times was its overtly aristocratic officer class. Promotion and success

for an officer depended on influence and, above all, on money. Gentlemen of the correct social background could, quite literally, buy their commissions and promotions. The 'purchase' system was finally abolished in 1872.

Purchase of commissions in the Army had a long history dating back to the reign of Edward VI, long before the regular army existed. Several attempts had been made to stamp it out and many Royal Commissions had reported on it. This attention seemed only to make it stronger and more entrenched. The Duke of Wellington favoured it. Like many others he felt that it ensured that officers came from the correct part of society.

In the 18th century it had been given official sanction and various restrictions on prices had been imposed. This completely failed to stop corrupt and incompetent officers from attaining high rank, at least up to lieutenant colonel, above which purchase was prohibited. Lord Cardigan was reputed to have paid £20,000 for the colonelcy of his regiment, the 11th Hussars. To buy in to some regiments, at the lowest commissioned rank of ensign, could cost the small fortune of £3,000 or more.

In the Crimean War in the 1850s the Army had proved to be ill-supplied with recruits and equipment and ill-served by its commanders and many untrained, effectively part-time, officers.

Reform was slow in coming and it was only in the 1870s that Edward Cardwell, the Secretary of State for War, swept through the Army and set it on a modern footing, much to the consternation of the old soldiers in command at 'Horse Guards' in London.

Amongst the reforms that were eventually passed through Parliament was a centralised, unified High Command, firmly subordinate to the Secretary of State and Parliament. Terms of service for soldiers were reduced and included several years 'in reserve', thus paving the way for an adequate reserve of trained men who could be called up if ever the need arose. Pairs of battalions were re-organised into formal regiments: one battalion would be on overseas service while its sister battalion was back at the home depot, recruiting and training for both of them. This period also saw the last of branding and tattooing as a form of punishment for desertion.

The one reform that caused the biggest problem was the 'abolition of purchase'. After a struggle in the House of Commons, Cardwell and his Prime Minister Gladstone had to wait for the vested interests in the House of Lords to do their worst. Most Tory peers who had any connections with the Army (which was most of them) had their say on the matter. Very few wanted change. Some supported the purchase system because it provided for a cheap form of retirement. Others supported it because it kept out 'the professional man with professional politics'. Yet more thought that the compensation required for existing holders of commissions, which would become unsaleable, would cost too much.

Gladstone in the end lost patience. It turned out that Parliamentary legislation was not needed anyway. At a stroke he altered *Queens Regulations*, which had provided the official sanction for the purchase system, and declared that from the following year, purchase would cease to exist. The Tories and the members of the House of Lords were furious but in the end there was nothing they could do. 'Purchase' ceased to exist on 1 November 1872. Compensation was paid, the total sum being in the region of £6 million – a large sum, even as the price of a fundamental reform.

–

The thought of buying promotion in today's Army, quite openly, seems ridiculous. As a system it enabled the mediocre to thrive as long as they were wealthy. On occasion it gave way to disaster. Yet paradoxically it was the same system that provided some vital, gallant leadership at some crucial moments in time of war.

74 The LAST of the Duchy of Lancaster

1873

The Lancaster estate was created by Henry III for his second son Edmund Crouchback. Later, in the 14th century, John of Gaunt, Edward III's son, became Duke of Lancaster through his wife's inheritance. Although John of Gaunt never became king, his son did – Henry IV. The Duchy of Lancaster thereafter became inextricably linked with the British Crown. The Duchy finally lost its real powers in 1873 when the Judicature Act removed the last of its responsibilities in exercising the criminal and civil law within its lands.

The Duchy of Lancaster consists of 21,000 hectares of land in the north of England; ironically most of this land is not in Lancashire but in Yorkshire. Until 1873, the Chancellor of the Duchy of Lancaster was responsible for a number of administrative and legal duties. This included the control of the law courts and the issue of rulings that the Lord Chancellor carried out for the rest of the country. From the appointment of the High Sheriff of Lancaster downwards, the Chancellor of the Duchy exercised his rights and privileges. In 1873 the Government decided to abolish this anomaly and incorporate the Duchy, for all practical purposes, into the rest of England. The position of Chancellor to the Duchy, however, was retained.

–

Today the Duchy of Lancaster still exists, the estate managed by the Crown on behalf of the Queen. The revenues from the Duchy form part of the contribution provided for the upkeep of the Sovereign. The Chancellor of the Duchy of Lancaster is a Government appointment, strictly political, its holder usually a member of the cabinet with some special responsibility appropriate to the politics of the day.

75 The LAST stage coaches

October 1874

Stage coaches have an important place in the reality and the romance of British history. Each bouncing, gaudily painted, fragile, enclosed carriage – its driver swaying on top, nobly controlling the straining horses – is a gem from the past. Stage coaches were overtaken, in more ways than one, by the technology of the Victorian age.

The stage coach had its golden period in Britain in the first few decades of the 19th century – it was developed further and lingered for much longer in the north. Regular services had been introduced in the 17th century and these were improved and augmented by the expansion of the turnpike roads and the increasing network of coaching inns. At the peak there were dozens of routes out of all major cities. The roads through most towns and villages throughout the United Kingdom were bustling with coach traffic running in all directions.

In the late 18th century some coach routes started to carry the Royal Mail, replacing the slower post-boys on horseback. The first such route was from London to Bristol in the West Country in 1784. Protected by armed guards, the Mail Coaches carried the post to all parts of Britain for over fifty years.

The railways arrived in the 1830s and within a few years were providing a superior, faster and more reliable service for both the passengers and the mail in much of southern Britain. The decay of the turnpike road system, deliberately encouraged by the rail lobby, did not help. The last Mail Coach service out of London closed down in 1846.

Further north the railways were not so dominant. The last great long-distance coach services, carrying the mail, were to be found in the Scottish Highlands. As the years of the century passed the railways spread throughout the country and, one by one, the coach services were replaced. The last long distance coach service, the *Royal Mail*, was from Inverness to Thurso. It ceased in the autumn of 1874, much regretted and mourned even in its day.

–

Today the romance of the days of coaching still lives. The love of horses, the coaching prints and the magic of 'Dickensian' style Christmas cards has burnished the folk memory of the forerunner of today's public transport system. The combination of fact, fiction and myth that surrounds the image of the stage coach remains a powerful one.

76 The LAST climbing boys

1875

One of the most iniquitous exploitations of children in the years up to and including the 19th century was by chimney sweeps. Young boys, small enough to ascend even the narrowest and most complex of flues, were sent up the chimneys to clean them. These 'climbing boys' as they were known were cheaper and easier to employ than any of the mechanical devices available. Their employment in Britain finally ceased in 1875 after a long campaign, a number of Acts of Parliament and many unnecessary deaths and injuries.

The champion of the climbing boys, ardent reformer and publicist of so many of the oppressing social problems of the day, was Lord Shaftesbury. Employment legislation of 1840 had outlawed the use of boys to climb chimneys but enforcement had proved almost impossible. Although certain philanthropic persons and organisations attempted to observe and report abuse it was necessary to have an eye-witness account of a boy actually entering or leaving a chimney before the local magistrates would act – not the sort of evidence that was easy to obtain. A further Children's Employment Act was passed in 1864 but, again, it failed to define who was to enforce it.

Occasionally notorious cases did come to court, usually because the climbing boy in question had been found dead – often trapped and suffocated in a difficult chimney. Sometimes boys were even burned to death – it was, after all, inconvenient to have to put a fire out just to have the chimney cleaned.

A case came to Shaftesbury's attention in 1872 that gave him the publicity to act. A seven-year old boy had died in a chimney and his master had been convicted and sentenced to six month's hard labour.

Three years later Parliament finally produced legislation which would work. All chimney sweeps would, from now on, require licences to carry out their trade. These licences were to be issued by the local police and needed to be renewed annually. Offending sweeps were deprived of their licences and livelihood.

–

The law of the land at last took over where before it had been left to volunteers. The days of the climbing boys were over.

77 The LAST marling gangs
1876

Before the advent of modern chemical fertilisers, farmers had to rely on more natural products to improve their soil. In Britain one of the fertilisers often used was marl, a clay mineral dug up by the marlers, itinerant gangs who would travel the countryside offering their services to farms. The practice died out in the 1870s.

Marl is a naturally occurring mixture of calcium carbonate and silt and it could be dug up in regions of clay soil. It was highly regarded as a fertiliser and was an important product – especially in wheat-growing regions.

The marling gangs with their elected leaders, or 'lords', had long established traditions and practices. They travelled from farm to farm discovering and obtaining the marl for the resident farmer. The marl was carted to and spread on the fields where it was required. Along with manure and imported potash it was one of the most important fertilisers available.

With the introduction of manufactured fertilisers, the so-called 'artificial manures', in the second half of the 19th century, marl was found to be much too expensive. Around 1876 the last of the gangs of marlers was disbanded.

Today their work can still be seen in the corners of some fields in the form of the pits they left behind. Inevitably overgrown, often filled with water, the marl pits are usually unnoticed by most passers by.

78 The LAST amateur FA Cup Final

9 April 1881

In football circles the Football Association Cup Final is the highlight of the season: the two best clubs meeting to battle it out for the sport's most coveted prize, the FA Cup. The Football Association was formed in 1863, the teams and players on the whole being ex-public school and amateur. An annual competition for the FA Cup was established in 1871. As more and more northern, semi-professional working class clubs joined the drift to professionalism accelerated. As far as the top teams were concerned, the amateur player gradually disappeared and the last FA Cup Final with two wholly amateur teams was played in 1881.

The last amateur team in a Football
Association cup final, the 'Challenge
Cup' of 1883. The Old Etonians were
appearing in their third consecutive
final but lost to the professional team,
Blackburn Olympic.

This particular Final took place at the Kennington Oval, in London, on 9 April. The Old Etonians played the Old Carthusians. 4,500 people watched the match which was won 3-0 by the Old Carthusians. Page, Wynard and Parry scored the goals.

The Old Etonians again played in the Final of 1882, against the professional Blackburn Rovers. They won 1-0 and thus became the last amateur team to win the FA Cup. Again in 1883 they appeared in the Final, this time against Blackburn Olympic; they lost but had the further distinction of being the last amateur side to reach the final.

The FA Cup Final was played at the Oval until 1892. It then was played at various sites, mainly Crystal Palace, until 1923 when it was moved to today's famous venue, Wembley.

79 The LAST flogging of soldiers and sailors

1881

The harsh conditions in both the British Army and Navy in the 19th century are generally well known. By today's standards, punishments for offenders against the rigorous discipline were brutal. The 'flogging round the fleet' of a mutinous sailor or the soldier lashed to a wheel and given 1,000 lashes for desertion were violent solutions in violent times. After a century of increasing public concern and the gradual introduction of more humane conditions of service, the last flogging of a British soldier took place in 1881.

In the Royal Navy, flogging members of the crew as a punishment was commonplace – although usually technically illegal. Captains were urged to restrict the number of lashes with the cat-o'-nine-tails on a seaman's bare back to no more than a dozen. This order was usually ignored: floggings of three or four dozen were more the norm than the exception. The offender was made to strip to the waist and was then lashed by his arms and feet to a grating or ladder. All hands were ordered on deck to witness the gruesome punishment with the company of Royal Marines standing by to maintain discipline.

The 'cat' was a multiple whip made of many leather thongs with knotted ends, frequently with lead shot attached to cause deeper cuts. Opportunities for sadism were obviously great – amongst the all-powerful captains as well as the boatswain's mates who were charged with actually swinging the cat. Some captains would give summary punishments, without trial, to members of his crew for relatively trivial offences such as 'sullenness' and perceived 'slowness' to react to orders. Others used it sparingly, but even as late as the 1850s many ships witnessed a flogging at least once a week, even in peacetime.

In the Army punishment was even more severe. Desertion – what today might be termed AWOL, merely 'absent without leave' – was rewarded by an official brutality which sanctioned hundreds of lashes to the offender's bare back. The victim was usually spreadeagled and tied to a triangular wooden frame. Traditionally, a drummer administered the blows supervised by the drum major, with the regimental doctor standing by to try to prevent a fatality. Offending soldiers were often maimed for life; many had to be discharged from service to almost certain penury and beggary in civilian life.

In the Navy the maximum number of permissible lashes for any flogging was reduced to forty-eight in 1866. A few years later, in 1871, it was suspended in peacetime and in 1879 officially abolished.

The soldiers in the Army had to suffer a few more years. In 1868, driven by the reforming zeal of Cardwell, the Secretary for War, the Army abolished flogging altogether in peacetime. Out too went the barbaric practice of branding or tattooing for desertion. Wars of course continued and thus in 1881 the last recorded official flogging took place.

–

In 1900 flogging in all the armed services was abolished even in war time. The new century brought in an age, which lasted until the First World War, of a highly trained, professional Army with very respectable conditions of service which at last extended to more humane punishments.

80 Anthony Trollope's LAST writing

1883

Anthony Trollope was one of the most distinguished, popular and prolific novelists of his day. He wrote and published over 50 novels, from 1847 until his death in December 1882. His last written work was *The Landleaguers*, a novel about the contemporary unrest in Ireland which was unfinished when he died.

A truly international man, Trollope's novels – with carefully constructed plots and lovingly created characters who often reappeared in several different stories – reflected his travels throughout Europe, America, the Middle East and Australia. But he is perhaps best known for his stories about the professional and landed classes of Victorian Britain. His church 'Barsetshire' novels and political 'Palliser' novels are memorials to sections of 19th century society that are still found fascinating and entertaining today.

It was appropriate however that his last novel, *The Landleaguers*, was about Ireland. His first published novel too had an Irish theme. He had worked in Banagher in Ireland for the Post Office in the 1840s and it was here that he had learned to love and enjoy life after an unhappy childhood and difficult, debt-ridden early days in London.

Unlike many of his fellow novelists of the time, Trollope usually had one or two completed books ready for publication while he was writing a new work. Many books, including his, were published as serials, in weekly or monthly parts; some authors wrote them virtually from week to week, often responding, in the plot, to public reactions – much as modern, so-called 'soap operas' are produced on television today. Trollope tried to avoid this pressure. Although a remorselessly disciplined and punctual writer (he wrote a regular 250 words on each page, every quarter of an hour, for three hours every morning), he was most uncomfortable with the idea of simultaneous writing and publication. With *The Landleaguers* he unfortunately found himself in this very position. Publication in the weekly journal *Life* began in November 1882, as he lay in a London nursing home, just a few days after a paralytic stroke. He never recovered and died on 6 December with only forty-nine of the planned sixty chapters completed.

—

The serial publication of *The Landleaguers* continued until October in the following year when it was then re-published in book form. His last complete published novel, in 1884, was *An Old Man's Love* which he had completed before he started *The Landleaguers*.

As far as his writing was concerned he was a self-demanding man; he had already meticulously prepared an autobiography, complete with instructions to his son to arrange for posthumous publication. This work ended with a valediction in which, 'from the further shore' he bid 'adieu to all who have cared to read any among the many words' that he had so lovingly written. He was much mourned by society and today his books are very much respected.

81 The LAST scaffold reprieve

February 1885

Old stories of last minute reprieves for condemned prisoners on the scaffold are legend. The story goes that if the hangman was unable to carry out his grim work on his victim, then, after the third attempt, the prisoner was allowed to live. True or false? – true! The last occasion when this happened was at Exeter jail in February 1885 when John Lee escaped the hangman's noose, living to tell his tale to astonished journalists and to many a fellow prisoner for years to come

Not many criminals who have been condemned to die survive to describe the awful experience of mounting the scaffold – but there were a few. An inefficient executioner, chopping a head off with an axe, had very little option but to carry on if the first blow did not achieve its intended swift purpose. With a hanging, if the rope broke, the scaffold collapsed or the trap door failed to open, a second or even third attempt could be carried out on the fully alive and aware victim.

In the rough and ready days of hangings, when some hangmen

were better than others, hangings were often – to put it simply – botched. It became a tradition that if the victim survived three attempts at being hanged, he would be reprieved, sometimes being granted freedom but more often having his sentence commuted to life imprisonment.

John Lee was a servant in Babbacombe in Devon. In November 1884 his employer, a Miss Keyse, was savagely beaten to death. Lee, protesting his innocence all the while, was convicted of her murder and condemned to death the following February.

On the day appointed for his execution he was bound and blindfolded by the hangman James Berry and led out from his cell. The hanging was to take place in the coach house. Instead of a scaffold there was a pit in the floor, some eleven feet deep, covered by trap doors which were operated by a lever.

Lee was positioned over the doors, the noose about his neck. He was calm and dignified. Asked if he had anything to say, he replied, 'No – drop away!' He held his breath, clenched his teeth and prepared to die.

Berry pulled the lever and to gasps of astonishment from the prison officials, there to witness the execution, nothing happened. Berry kept pulling – still nothing.

Lee had the noose removed from his neck and was led away into the next room while the trap doors were tested. They seemed to work well, with no-one on them.

Lee was brought back and again prepared to meet his maker. Again the executioner tugged at the lever and once again the trap doors refused to drop away. The officials decided to postpone the execution again, but Lee – perhaps with a traditional reprieve in mind – insisted on a third attempt. It was made and again to no avail.

The prison chaplain could now bear it no longer and decided to leave. An execution had to be witnessed by the chaplain and so without him the proceedings had to be stopped anyway. Lee was led away to his cell to wait the whole day in dreadful uncertainty.

Late that evening the governor visited him. The message was that he was to live! He was officially reprieved and would have his sentence commuted to a life term.

–

There were no more such reprieves; the prison authorities learned their lesson from the incident at Exeter and built their scaffolds with more care. John Lee spent twenty-three years in jail, before walking out a free man.

82 The LAST voyage of the SS *Great Britain*
24 May 1886

Launched in 1843, the brainchild of the great Victorian engineer Isambard Kingdom Brunel, the *SS Great Britain* was a ship of truly revolutionary design. She was large, exceptionally well-built and the first ship constructed entirely of iron and driven by a propeller to cross the Atlantic. She was conceived as a ship to compete against the regular American packet ships which crossed the ocean on schedule and with a fair amount of comfort. Her last commercial voyage ended in the Falkland Islands in May 1886.

American ships had held a near monopoly of the passenger trade between New York and Liverpool for some thirty years. Brunel and his Great Western Steamship Company planned to change all this. The *Great Western* – his first attempt, a paddle ship – had already proved that steam power could provide a more reliable service than sail.

The *Great Britain* was 322 feet in overall length with a width of 50 feet 6 inches. Her gross tonnage was 3,270. The ship was a sensation wherever she went throughout the 1840s, 1850s and even 1860s. Her size and beauty were remarkable enough but technically she outshone all other ships for many years. The *Great Britain* originally was designed as steamer, with auxiliary sail to help save on coal whenever the wind was favourable. She had six masts – one was square rigged, the other five had fore-and-aft sails. She underwent many changes throughout her life and ended her career as a pure sailing ship with three masts, all square rigged – an ironic reversion to an old design for such a famous, revolutionary ship.

Designed to carry up to 360 passengers and 600 tons of cargo, the *Great Britain* had an exceptionally long and industrious career, under many different owners, from the pioneering trans-Atlantic passenger travel in the 1840s to the transportation of immigrants and cargo to Australia for some twenty years. In 1855 during the Crimean war she was used as a troop ship carrying, on several voyages, thousands of soldiers to the Crimea and to ports in the Mediterranean area. She was also pressed into service two years later to help out in the Indian Mutiny. She made the voyage from Ireland, around the Cape of Good Hope, to Bombay in seventy days, carrying several regiments to help in suppressing the Mutiny. She ended her sea-going career on voyages carrying coal from Wales to the west coast of the United States of America.

It was on such a trip that she ended her commercial sea-going life. The crew numbered thirty-seven and the master was fifty-three year old Captain Stap.

Rounding the Horn, on the southern tip of South America is still a maritime adventure today. In 1886, Cape Horn and a strong westerly gale proved too much for a large, leaky, fully laden old sailing ship. The coal cargo shifted and the ship was listing badly before the crew managed to shovel it back again. Her fore and main top mast were lost in the winds and the crew fought for many hours to cut the old rigging free. The deck planking leaked badly and the fresh water tanks were contaminated with sea water. After more than a month of struggling in the mountainous seas of the South Atlantic, her Captain finally succumbed to repeated requests from the crew to turn back. On 13 May the *Great Britain* was turned around and ran for cover to Port Stanley in the British colony of the Falkland Islands.

The indignities to the old ship were not yet over. She ran aground twice at the harbour entrance and was finally towed in on 24 May 1886. After many months of hard bargaining, with all the crew eventually paid off, the Falklands Island Company bought her for use as a floating store ship.

Slowly disintegrating, the *Great Britain* – floating in Port Stanley Harbour – became part of the scenery for generations of locals and visitors. In 1937 she was too old even for storage of the bales of wool from Falkland Islands sheep. She was towed a few miles away to Sparrow Cove, beached and left to rot.

–

But that was not the end for the *Great Britain*. After many years of lobbying from the USA and Britain she was rescued from her near grave. In 1970 she was floated onto a pontoon and towed from the

South Atlantic to her birthplace in England, at Bristol's Great Western Dry Dock, where she rests today, a permanent ship museum, a monument to an extraordinary 19th century maritime vision.

83 Jack the Ripper's LAST victim

9 November 1888

The Whitechapel Murderer, or 'Jack the Ripper' as he called himself in his taunting letters to the police, was responsible for a series of horrifying murders in the east end of London. They shocked everyone, even those who were used to the daily routine of criminal violence in Victorian cities. His victims were all women and the bodies were all brutally, disgustingly disfigured. He was never caught and certainly went to his death, by whatever means, unidentified as the cause of one of the greatest criminal legends ever. His last victim, Marie Jeanette Kelly, met her gruesome end in November 1888. She was the most severely mutilated of all.

Jack the Ripper is a name that is synonymous with the most vile of criminals, the unpredictable, unbalanced, unhinged and, above all, unidentified multi-murderer. In the summer and autumn of 1888 the public waited with breath held for news of the next victim. As each mutilated body was found, tension among the police grew amid increasingly shrill public exhortation to find the perpetrator of such ghastly crimes.

In the maze of the overcrowded east end of London in the 1880s the police were seemingly helpless in their attempts to track down, identify and arrest the Ripper.

Many suggestions as to the Ripper's identity were made, both at the time and throughout the more than hundred years since, but it has to be admitted that the Ripper was never identified and never caught. Many murders were attributed to him (or even her, as some have claimed) but it is now commonly believed that he was only definitely responsible for the murder of five of the women.

The first of the Ripper's victims was found in Whitechapel, in the east end of London; this and all the subsequent murders were thus initially referred to as the 'Whitechapel' murders even though the last four took place in Spitalfields to the north of Whitechapel. After his second victim was discovered the murderer wrote a mocking letter to the police and signed himself 'Jack the Ripper'. Thus the name was born, to haunt the police and public and remind them for ever of the fallibility of crime detection.

Spitalfields was an area in London of closely packed houses, frequented by the lowest criminals and dregs of Victorian metropolitan society. Prostitutes plied their trade here and it was exclusively among them that the Ripper selected his unfortunate victims.

Marie Jeanette Kelly was a twenty-five year old Irish prostitute who lived in Dorset Street. Like all prostitutes in the area she was disturbed and frightened by the Ripper affair and was actually planning to leave London for a while until he had been caught.

On the evening of 8 November, after many hours of drinking and plying her trade, Marie Kelly picked up her last customer. The next morning, 9 November, she was found horribly murdered, mutilated, disemboweled and partially dismembered, nearly beyond recognition.

Three days later the Metropolitan Police Commissioner, Sir Charles Warren, admitting the failure of his force, resigned. Kelly proved to be the last of the Ripper's victims, although this was not realised at the time and many subsequent murders were initially attributed to him.

—

The Ripper's file was kept open, officially, until 1892. In the interval since then hundreds of books have been written on the subject, many of them claiming to reveal the true identity of the Ripper. Many thousands of documents and photographs have come to light, but there has yet to be a convincing, conclusive story which encompasses the full facts and lays bare the real truth of Jack the Ripper.

84 The LAST of the crinoline and the bustle

1889

Ladies' fashions of the 19th century were epitomised by the awesome sight of the huge bell-shape of the crinoline dress. The skirts, laid over several layers of petticoats supported by a cage, came right down to the ground, covering even the lady's footwear. The crinoline was later replaced by the bustle, a strategically positioned bulge at the rear of the waist. These extraordinary devices finally disappeared from the fashionable scene in 1889.

Victorian ladies, dressed in their cumbersome finery, seem to dominate the formal posed photographs of the period. From Queen Victoria downwards, all ladies of means wore hugely supported dresses, almost completely concealing their figures. A stranger to the scene might have wondered whether these Victorian ladies had any legs at all.

A framework of hoops underneath the dresses was the secret. Originally they were made of horsehair and linen but this was soon replaced by whalebone or steel. The style was first dome-shaped and then in the 1860s became more pyramidal. In this period, when crinoline dresses were at their largest, it would have been difficult to find anything less practical for women to wear for every day use. But wear them they did, and today they remind us that blind devotion to the heights of fashion is nothing new. Some of the particular varieties of crinoline shapes had peculiar names such as 'cage américaine', 'ondina' and 'sansflectum'.

Gradually some kind of practical sense began to prevail in the late-1860s: the front of the crinoline dress became flatter, the rear pushed out even more, taking the burden both of perceived beauty and of fashion. The rearwards movement of the crinoline over several years resulted in the recall of the bustle, a cage attached to the back of the petticoat to push out the dress. This modified crinoline was referred to as a crinolette. Later the bustle proper, a separate wad of padding tied around the waist with tapes, held the dress out to the required shape. Sometimes the skirt at the back was made to stand out at a right angle, forming a small platform.

THE NEW

Canfields

BUSTLE
FOR THE **MILLION**

So arranged with a spring as to fold up when wearer is sitting or lying down, the Bustle resuming its proper position upon rising.

Size can be altered by means of an adjustable cord.

Light, cool, easy to wear, never gets out of order, and is the correct Parisian shape. Best Bustle to fit a dress over. The only Bustle ever made to fit any lady and every dress.

By Royal Letters Patent, No. 6,043.

Depth, including band, 11 in

OF ALL DRAPERS AND LADIES' OUTFITTERS
THROUGHOUT THE KINGDOM.

Price 2s. 6d.

By post 3d. extra. Send Stamps or Postal Order.
WHOLESALE ONLY

STAPLEY and SMITH,

LONDON WALL, LONDON, E.C.

The secret of the bustle is revealed. An advertisement for the 'New Canfield Bustle' shows its mechanical intricacies, with the small print hinting that the wearer was even able to sit down in comfort. The bustle disappeared rapidly after the 1889 season.

–

1889 was the last year when the bustle itself could be worn fashionably. Women needed to move about a lot more, to do more things – even the wealthy ones. A more practical approach began to creep into ladies' fashions. Slimmer, sleeker dresses – displaying the figure more fully – were the rage by the end of the century.

85 The LAST duke

29 July 1889

In the hierarchy of the aristocracy no-one apart from royalty, comes higher than a duke. In these days of equality the creation of new peerages in Britain is, with a few notable exceptions, limited to life peers. These are barons, the lowest of the five ranks of 'lord', created only for their lifetime and unable to transfer the honour to their descendants when they die. Not so the hereditary peerages; and certainly not the dukes. Outside the relatively common creations for royal princes, the last creation of a duke was in 1889.

In the creation of dukedoms, however, nothing helps more than a proximity to the royal family. The last creation was no exception; so, when in 1889 Her Royal Highness the Princess Louise, twenty-two year old daughter of the Prince of Wales, grand-daughter of Queen Victoria, married the forty year old Alexander Duff, Marquess of Macduff, from County Banff, Ireland, a suitable wedding present was not slow in arriving.

Two days later the Marquess became the Duke of Fife and Britain's last dynasty of dukes was created. This creation was, it must be admitted, only an Irish one, so in 1900 the Duke of Fife was promoted to a Duke of the United Kingdom. His descendant, the current Duke of Fife, remains last in the list of seniority of Dukes of the United Kingdom.

–

The interesting side to this dukedom did not end there. It descended to the present Duke through the female line. The first Duke had no sons but in honour of his wife (created Princess Royal in 1905) it was decreed that on his death his daughters could succeed. This they duly did. His eldest, Princess Alexandra, became Duchess of Fife in her own right. On her death (to complicate matters even further) her son, already Duke of Connaught from his grandfather (Arthur Duke of Connaught, Queen Victoria's son) did not become Duke of Fife. That honour passed to her nephew, her younger sister's son. He became known as the third Duke of Fife, his aunt the Duchess being the second Duke.

When, in 1955, Sir Winston Churchill retired as Prime Minister he was offered a dukedom, probably the very last to have had that offer. The 'Duke of London' was the suggested title. He refused as it would have been a 'blight on the prospects' of the political careers of his son Randolph and his grandson Winston. They would have been unable to sit in the House of Commons when they, in turn, inherited the title.

86 The LAST bare knuckle prizefighting

8 July 1889

Prizefighting was a sport with its origins in the mists of time. In Britain it developed into a popular racy spectator sport, with heavy side betting, in the 18th century. By the Regency period it had achieved a certain respectability with patronage from the highest echelons of royalty downwards. Bare knuckle fights were beginning to be considered dangerous by the 1870s and were gradually replaced by more formal fights, with padded gloves, under the Marquess of Queensberry's rules. The last recognised bare knuckle fight in Britain was for the heavyweight championship in 1885. By 1889, the year of the last recognised international bare knuckle contest ever, in Belgium, the days of rough prizefighting were over.

Boxing as we know it today developed out of bare knuckle prizefighting as fought in England in the 1830s. Regulations for conducting these bloody battles, which went on for as long as the contestants could stand up unaided, were stipulated in the so-called London Prize Ring Rules. By 1838 these were accepted in the USA and on the continent of Europe. The longest fight on record was in Cheshire, where a 276 round contest lasted a gruelling four and a half hours before the victor was decided. Short fights occurred too, one fight lasted for a mere seven seconds. By the time of the first recognised 'World Title' fight in 1860 (in England between local boy Tom Sayers and John C. Heenan of the USA), which was declared a draw after thirty-seven rounds, the new rules were beginning to spread. In 1867 the sporting aristocrat the Marquess of Queensberry had devised a formal set of rules, initially for amateurs but soon adopted by professionals.

The main stipulation of the new rules was that the fighters would wear gloves, the count of ten was introduced for a knock down and behaviour in the ring was more rigorously controlled. For some years these rules were used as well as the London Prize Ring Rules; indeed many fighters fought under both rules at different times in different fights.

The authorities were beginning to clamp down on bare knuckle fighting however. In America it was quite common for the the police to step in to stop a fight, if the referee refused to do so. Several fighters were prosecuted for assault.

The last British bare knuckle prize fight took place in London on 17 December 1885. Jem Smith beat Jack Davies to a bloody pulp to retain his heavyweight title. Smith later went on to fight and beat Frank Slavin at Bruges in Belgium in 1889 – in the very last internationally recognised glove-less prizefight ever staged.

The closing stages of the bare knuckle world championship were, appropriately enough, fought out in the USA. Jem Smith of England had fought Jake Kilrain for the world championship in France in 1887. The result, after a brisk 106 rounds, was declared a draw as the light began to fade. In the States, 'Boston Strong Boy' John L Sullivan was the recognised number one contender and, tempted by a $10,000 purse offered by the proprietor of the *Police Gazette*, agreed to fight Kilrain. Because Kilrain had already fought England's Jem Smith, admittedly resulting in a draw, the winner of the contest was to be declared the undisputed world champion.

The fight was held on 8 July 1889, at Richburg in Mississipi. It attracted great crowds. Spectators travelled from miles around by special trains. It lasted a mere two hours and sixteen minutes. Kilrain's seconds threw in the sponge after seventy-five rounds and John L Sullivan was declared the winner and world heavyweight bare knuckle champion.

–

Sullivan went on to make many appearances at demonstration fights all over the USA. When the more organised boxing matches began, Sullivan was defeated in the very first championship fight against 'Gentleman' Jim Corbett in 1892.

87 The LAST of Great Scotland Yard

1890

Scotland Yard is a name that is almost exclusively used to describe the headquarters of London's Metropolitan Police Force. Yet it was and is simply a place in London, just off Whitehall, where in 1829 space was found for the original offices of 'A' division of the newly formed Metropolitan Police. It soon became the headquarters for the entire London Metropolitan Force and in 1890 the 'Met' moved from Great Scotland Yard to new, purpose-built headquarters near Westminster Bridge. Although this was the last association it had with Great Scotland Yard, the Metropolitan Police Force used the name for its new building, New Scotland Yard, and it has been with it ever since, a name that is probably one of the most famous in law enforcement throughout the world.

In mediaeval times the kings of Scotland used travel to London to pay homage to the English kings for their English feudal holdings of Huntingdon and Cumberland. They stayed in buildings near the English court which forever after became known as 'Scotland' Yard. By the 18th century the small streets in the area were named Great Scotland Yard, Middle Scotland Yard and Little Scotland Yard.

When Sir Robert Peel as Home Secretary formed the London Metropolitan Police Force in 1829, a station for 'A' division was required. In Whitehall Place a row of small houses had been built a few years before. Number Four was vacant so permission was obtained to move in. The rear entrance to Number Four came out in Great Scotland Yard and, as this became the more used entrance, it gave its name to the building, then to the offices and eventually to the complete edifice of the headquarters operation of the entire Metropolitan Police.

The organisation outgrew its original building and by the 1870s there was an urgent need for more space. The Thames Embankment was in the process of construction and a site near the river which had originally been planned as a Grand National Opera House became available.

In 1884 a bomb planted by Irish Fenians blew in one of the walls at Great Scotland Yard and completely wrecked a public house across the road. Great Scotland Yard survived but its connection with the Met was nearly over. The police eventually moved out to their New Scotland Yard in 1890.

New Scotland Yard, the institution, outgrew its 1890 building too and in 1967 moved to its present site in Victoria Street. The old New Scotland Yard was refurbished as extra offices for the nearby House of Parliament and was renamed the Norman Shaw Building, after the original architect.

Middle and Little Scotland Yard have long gone but the old Great Scotland Yard still survives, next to Whitehall Place, the address of various small government departments.

88 The LAST of the broad gauge

21 May 1892

During the 19th century Britain led the industrial world in many fields, no more so than in the area of railway engineering. In the 1830s and 1840s Isambard Kingdom Brunel had left the railway world gasping – in some cases spluttering – with his brilliance and vision as chief designer for the Great Western Railway. Always controversial, one of his main features for the Great Western, perhaps his most daring, was the seven foot 'broad' gauge of the railway tracks.

Most other railway companies, and there were several spread throughout mainland Britain, were content to go along with the more common, narrow width of 4 foot 8 and a half inches.

Brunel had always thought a wider gauge would be superior; not merely because the ride would be smoother and more comfortable. It was really a matter of engineering efficiency.

Friction was the greatest obstacle to higher speeds (forty miles per hour was considered fantastically fast) and reduction of running costs. Friction could be reduced by having larger wheels. Larger wheels meant higher, less stable carriages unless they could be mounted between the wheels instead of above them; at a gauge of seven feet this became possible without reducing carriage width. In fact, Great Western carriages were still wider than others and consequently very popular with passengers.

By the 1880s the Great Western Railway was running a large network throughout the south, the west and the south midlands of England and in South Wales. Their Bristol and Exeter track was served by their fastest locomotives and had, in the 1840s, provided the first 'express trains' in the world.

But technical superiority was not enough. From the start, the great inconvenience of the broad gauge system, that of its incompatibility with the rest of the railways, was a major problem. Passions ran high whenever there were discussions on the merits of different gauges – and broad gauge devotees were always the loudest in the arguments. Broad gauge was doomed just a few years after its inauguration when the folly of having differing systems was realised. Much of Great Western's own track and rolling stock was already narrow gauge by the 1880s. Most of their track had been given a third rail, 'mixed gauge', so that both narrow and broad gauge could use the same line. In 1861 they were already running their own narrow gauge trains from Paddington to Reading. Much of their rolling stock was designed so that it could later be easily converted to narrow gauge.

The last stretches of track that were still purely broad gauge were found on the Exeter to Truro main line and its branch lines. Much of the line was single track, so working on one line while another was still in use would have been impossible. It was decided that this last broad gauge stretch would be converted to narrow gauge over one single weekend, 21 and 22 May 1892. A track conversion team of 5,000 specially trained men was readied for the occasion.

On Friday 21 May, the last broad gauge passenger train, the *Cornishman*, left Paddington at 10.15am amid much ceremony. Crowds had gathered to see it leave and thousands lined the track all the way to Penzance. Many a coin was placed on the track to be flattened as a memento. West of Exeter the station masters received certificates authorising work to start immediately on the down track. The train reached Penzance at 8.20pm and began its return, now empty of passengers, at 9.10pm. It stopped at every station to Exeter and then steamed off to await its turn to be broken up at the Great Western's works at Swindon.

At daylight the next day the track team swung into action. The conversion was done without a hitch – thirty hours later the west country broad gauge track had gone. On Sunday night the mail train from Paddington ran on schedule – on narrow gauge.

–

So the narrow gauge won in the end. It had originally been chosen in the early part of the century, having gradually developed out of the early horse drawn colliery railways in the north of England. 4 foot 8 inches then seemed a naturally suitable width for these horse carts on tracks. Today the same gauge is used throughout many parts of the world and has even undergone metrification – it is now regarded as the international standard of 1432 mm.

89 The LAST steam-powered flight
31 July 1894

Steam-powered heavier-than-air flying seems such an outrageous, anachronistic dead-end in the development of the aeroplane that it is difficult now to believe that it actually did take place. The last recorded successful attempt at flight using steam power was in England in 1894. The experimenter was none other than Sir Hiram Maxim, American born, naturalised Briton, already famous as the inventor of the Maxim machine gun.

During the latter half of the 19th century numerous attempts at flying in the USA, France and Britain involved the use of steam power. Many of these experiments used models but a small number actually achieved a limited success in manned flight; perhaps powered 'hops' would be a more accurate description but they certainly attained some sort of aeronautical mobility.

One of the most notable successes was in France in 1890. Clément Ader constructed his 'bat-wing' style monoplane *Eole*

The fashionable set pay a visit to Baldwyns Park to marvel at Maxim's extraordinary flying machine. Maxim proved that powered flight was possible, but his huge aircraft – powered by a 300 horse power steam engine – was uncontrollable in the air and could fly only along special rails. Maxim's experiments were the last steam-powered attempts to fly. With the rapid development of the smaller, more efficient internal combustion engine smaller aircraft were soon to achieve successful controlled flight.

relying on an ingeniously designed steam engine which produced twenty horse power. It flew a series of short flights, not long enough to be categorised as completely successful, but it was certainly the very first aeroplane to take off under its own power.

Steam power, however, was by this time already obsolescent. The first internal combustion engines had been built in the 1870s and were far more promising as a potential source of power for a heavier-than-air aircraft.

Sir Hiram Maxim was one of those archetypal 'inventors' of the period and had turned his attention to flying machines in the 1880s. Careful experiments with wind tunnels had produced designs for aerofoils and propellers. An extremely efficient power plant, driven by steam, was designed to power an enormous biplane. With two gigantic propellers, the aircraft was designed to run along 1800 feet of railway track constructed at Baldwyns Park. An extra set of guide rails was fitted to prevent it leaving the track entirely.

After several experimental runs success came on 31 July 1894. Sir Hiram, with an additional two crew members on board, finally got his aeroplane, puffing and steaming, to lift off after a 600 foot run.

But this huge machine was only ever intended as a test rig. It would have been impossible to control it in free flight. Many demonstration runs followed, but with parts of the outer wing panels removed to prevent proper flight.

–

Unfortunately Sir Hiram then abandoned aviation for many years, to return only after the Wright brothers had made history with their own biplane, powered by their own power plant. This time it was a modern internal combustion engine which eventually gave the vital contribution to successful powered flight.

90 The LAST Prime Minister in the House of Lords

1895-1902

Robert Cecil, 3rd Marquess of Salisbury, was the last serving Prime Minister in the House of Lords. He was the Conservative leader for twenty years and on 25 June 1895 he formed his last Ministry.

Lord Robert Cecil was born the second son of the Marquess of Salisbury. As a young man, in 1850 after leaving Oxford University, Cecil spent two years on a round-the-world tour. His first hand view of the Empire in the making stood him in good stead throughout his life. On his return he was elected unopposed to the House of Commons as MP for Stamford in 1853. He succeeded to the marquesate on the death of his father in 1868, his elder brother having died earlier.

Before he first became Prime Minister, in 1885, Salisbury served in the India Office and also as Foreign Secretary. He had been out of office for three years when in 1895 his last Ministry was formed after the short-lived Liberal administration of Lord Rosebery. In fact, with a few short breaks, Salisbury dominated the political leadership of the country from 1885 until 1902 when, his health failing, he was persuaded to resign.

He was a true Victorian. Born fifteen years after the battle of Waterloo – he had the Duke of Wellington as his godfather – he died in 1902 a year after the end of the Boer War. He was not greatly in favour of the parliamentary reforms passed during his career and, despite being known for his 'masterly inactivity', he was a successful and much admired politician. He was also his own Foreign Secretary for much of his time as Premier. At a time of tremendous power and splendour for the British Empire he yet managed a foreign policy that was summed up in his own words: 'splendid isolation'.

He was a man of many talents, taking a keen interest in farming and above all scientific experimentation in the true Victorian style. When first called upon to form a Ministry it is said that the telegraph summoning him to the Queen at Balmoral interrupted him in his laboratory at Hatfield House whilst testing a telephone. It is fitting that someone who had made it a practice, throughout his career to resist much of the inevitable political change in Britain should have been the last non-elected prime minister.

Although most prime ministers since Salisbury have been elevated to the peerage after their time at 10 Downing Street, they were always members of the House of Commons whilst in office. There is no absolute constitutional requirement for such an arrangement but the general march of democracy since the end of the 19th century made it accepted practice. A prime minister who neither has submitted to the will of the electorate nor is able to speak in the House of Commons – the accepted source of real democratic authority – would now be completely unacceptable to the majority of the country.

In 1963 Prime Minister Macmillan resigned. On his advice to the Queen, Alec Douglas-Home, although in the House of Lords, was chosen to succeed him. The 14th Earl of Home – because of a change in the law earlier that year – was able to renounce his peerage. He fought and won a by-election to become a member of Parliament and to take up the reins of power at Number 10.

91 The LAST turnpike

1895

Turnpike roads were toll roads run by private companies, the Turnpike Trusts. They enabled the improvement of some roads which would otherwise have been left undeveloped – and thereby allowed a fast coaching service to be established in the 18th century. They encountered severe competition in the 1830s when the railways started to expand rapidly throughout Britain. The turnpikes gradually faded in importance during the rest of the century, many falling into disuse, and the last Turnpike Trust, in Angelsey, abolished its tolls in 1895.

The name turnpike comes from the 'pike', or bar, which was 'turned', acting as a gate to let the traveller pass after the toll had been paid. They were originally set up by an Act of 1663 which empowered magistrates to erect gates and charge a fee to anyone travelling over a given stretch of road by horse or carriage. Later, trust companies were created to manage the roads and to ensure that they were adequately repaired and maintained. Never popular, always accused of overcharging for the use of poorly kept roads, the Turnpike Trusts in their heyday controlled about six per cent of Britain's roads. There were 21,000 miles and 8,000 toll gates. 1871 saw the last toll roads in London.

–

Ironically, just as motor vehicles started to appear the last turnpike roads disappeared. The development of an adequate road system for a modern age was left to the central and local government authorities. Most UK roads are still free of tolls with the exception of some motorway bridges and tunnels. Throughout the country the turnpikes have left a legacy of the toll houses – which can still often be seen, usually beside a once important road junction – where the toll gate keepers used to live.

92 The LAST of the redcoats

January 1896

The beginning of the year saw the launch of a military campaign in West Africa against the Ashantis. It was typical of the small colonial wars of the latter part of the 19th century. It was also the last campaign in which the British Army wore its famous red tunic uniforms.

The story of the Army's transition from brightly coloured uniforms to today's camouflaged smocks is a long one. As far back as the 1800s in the Peninsular Campaign of the Napoleonic wars, it was realised by many commanders that clothing that allowed the wearer an opportunity to blend in with his background gave him a considerable advantage over the enemy.

In the middle of the 19th century, regular British units on the North-West Frontier in India had already started wearing 'khaki' (a Persian word for 'dusty') jackets. The move was not without its opponents. Many generals resisted with scorn and bitterness. Queen Victoria was also known to be against it.

By the last decades of the century, in the 1880s and 1890s, most British regiments had been kitted out with the more soberly coloured uniforms in which to fight. On being sent off on campaigns they normally put their red tunics and fancy headgear into mothballs before marching off to battle, attired in sober khaki outfits.

At the end of 1895 the warriors of the Ashanti Kingdom were once again terrorising the British territory of the Gold Coast in West Africa. Twenty years earlier Wolseley had been sent out to crush this troublesome nation. Now they would have to sorted out once and for all.

An ultimatum was sent to their King Prempeh but no answer was received.

A force of some 2,000 men was despatched from Cape Coast Castle in December under the command of General Scott. The main regular British unit involved was the 2nd Battalion of the West Yorkshire Regiment. The remainder of the force was made up of supporting arms and native units.

They marched inland, hacking their way through the thick jungle, eventually arriving at the Ashanti capital of Kumasi in January 1986. Here they found the King who, despite the fearsome reputation of his warriors, spent most of his time in an alcoholic stupor. Resistance was slight and fighting was brief. The King was deposed and deported to the coast, replaced by that ubiquitous and all important member of the Empire, the British Resident, to govern in his place.

There were no dramatic battles in this campaign. The 'thin red line' did not disappear for ever behind lines of smoking rifles and bellowed commands above the din of battle. These last campaigning redcoats, the West Yorkshires, were well organised on a methodical and professional campaign – perhaps a more fitting tribute.

–

Today, apart from military bandsmen, the Household Division of the British Army the 'Guards' are the only soldiers regularly to wear red jackets and dark blue trousers on parade. The annual event of Trooping the Colour at Horse Guards in London is appreciated by the public in their thousands.

93 The LAST of the 'Red Flag' Act

13 November 1896

1896 was a year that was crucial to the development of the motor car in Britain. The abolition of the so-called 'Red Flag' Act of 1865 brought an end to the restrictions placed on mechanical transport, including the new 'horseless carriages'.

For most of the latter half of the century the railways provided the supreme method of efficient long distance travel. People of all classes could ride in relative comfort, for little cost, to all parts of the country. The stage coaches and associated hostelries of Pickwickian travel belonged to the distant past and the road system had deteriorated badly. What roads there were outside the towns had been neglected and were suitable only for country folk for local travelling about their business.

Rather than repair and maintain the roads, the Government tried to restrict their use. Motorised transport, steam traction engines and some other steam carriages were severely limited by the passing of the 'Red Flag' Act of 1865. This restricted speeds to four miles per hour and required the vehicle to be preceded by a walking man carrying a red flag. There probably was some danger – to passengers and others – in travelling too fast, but pressure from the railway owners had a not inconsiderable influence in getting this Act onto the statute books.

In Germany in 1885 Benz invented his motor car and in 1894 the first of the new fangled machines from Germany and France began to be imported into Britain by intrepid 'motorists'. By this time the red flag of the 'Red Flag Act' had been abolished but the speed limit of four miles per hour and the man on foot still remained in law. What was suitable for slow moving, steam-driven contraptions was clearly inappropriate for the modern motor car of the 1890s. Something had to be done to help the fledgling motor industry, despite a general resistance from the establishment to these dangerous 'horseless carriages'.

Pressure on the Government to change the law came from several quarters. One of them was Harry Lawson, a colourful entrepreneur who recognised the potential for motor cars if only they could be given unrestricted access to the country's highways.

155

He really did seem to appreciate how the motor car could develop and radically affect the transport system forever. At last the Government relented. It was agreed that the speed limit would be raised to fourteen miles per hour (to be lowered by local government boards to twelve miles per hour) and the necessity for a foot man would be abolished.

The new Locomotives on Highways Act came into force in November. 13 November was the last day on which motorists were restricted to four miles per hour. On 14 November, in celebration, Harry Lawson organised the first of the 'London to Brighton' runs that are still an annual event today. Thirty cars took part and with some foresight Lawson told those who reached Brighton that history would remember their 'immortal ride'.

–

The British motor industry began to develop almost immediately. By the end of the century, just a few years later, Britain could boast dozens of firms in the car making business competing with the best that the continental and American firms could offer.

94 Gladstone's LAST speech

September 1896

William Ewart Gladstone was one of those few politicians whose active life nearly spanned the century and whose political activities covered a major portion of it. His powers of oratory were tremendous; his ability to control his audiences with his skills as a speaker was recognised before he even entered Parliament. His last public political speech was given in Liverpool, in 1896, a year after he had retired from the House of Commons.

Christianity dominated Gladstone's own life; that domination combined with the inconvenience of his powerful conscience would have troubled any lesser politician. He was member of Parliament for over sixty-three years, from 1833 to 1895. He first entered Parliament representing the 'pocket borough' of Newark as a Tory. As one of the 'Peelites' he later joined with the Whigs to form the Liberal party.

He sat in ten cabinets, four of them as Prime Minister. He was, in his later years, referred to by his political friends as the 'Grand Old Man', or G.O.M. Unlike his great rival, the flamboyant Disraeli, Gladstone had a cool, unfriendly relationship with Queen Victoria. She responded to his simple and serious manners with a frosty, unfriendly detachment and, ultimately, with unkindness.

Gladstone spent much of the latter part of his political life fighting for Home Rule for Ireland – but this was not to be. By 1894 his health was fading, he suffered from deafness and his sight was poor. After resigning as Prime Minister in 1894 and relinquishing his seat in the House of Commons a year later, he retired to his country home of Hawarden in Wales.

In September 1896, the Turkish massacres in Armenia brought him out of retirement for a speech in Liverpool. At the age of eighty-six Gladstone gave an hour and a half of ringing denouncement of Abdul Hamid, the Sultan of Turkey, for his cruelty. With extraordinary foresight, in a curious preview of many of the international speeches of today's world leaders, he declared: 'The ground on which we stand is not British, nor European, but human.'

Gladstone died in May 1898 of a painful cancer of the mouth. His family were all present, kneeling around his bed as prayers were read for him. His death was treated with enormous reverence by all members of the political community. Tributes flowed from colleagues and opposition alike. He was a simple but great man.

95 The LAST Gilbert & Sullivan operetta

March 1896

The names Gilbert and Sullivan conjure up memories of a partnership that produced a glittering list of comic operettas in the late 19th century. The productions that they wrote together, William Gilbert the librettist, Arthur Sullivan the composer, have become classics. Most of them were originally staged by

the impresario Richard D'Oyly Carte and were the talk of the town in the 1870s and 1880s. They have enjoyed considerable success, being staged worldwide by amateurs and professionals ever since. After a stormy relationship, worthy to be a melodrama set to music in its own right, the last operetta that Gilbert and Sullivan wrote together was *The Grand Duke*, staged at the Savoy Theatre in 1896.

Near the beginning of their exceptionally successful partnership Gilbert had declared, with typical Victorian aplomb, that 'Sullivan and I intend to produce comic operas to which any man may bring his mother and his aunts.' After a long collaboration stretching from their first success, *Trial by Jury* in 1875, to *The Yeomen of the Guard* in 1889, they fell out bitterly during the writing of *The Gondoliers*. Sullivan had tired of light opera and was looking for fresh musical fields in which to graze. Gilbert was quite happy to continue as before. Eventually they quarreled over expenses, most ignobly over £500 spent on carpets at the new Savoy Theatre.

After a long and, it now seems, extremely childish argument, conducted mainly by letter, the two were reconciled in 1893 to write *Utopia Limited*. At the first performance they shook hands publicly to great applause. The opera itself was not a success and the two friends drifted apart again. Finally in 1895 Gilbert came to Sullivan with his outline plot for the last of their joint operas, *The Grand Duke*.

Sullivan, by now Sir Arthur Sullivan, agreed to write the score and *The Grand Duke*, or *The Statutory Duel*, opened at the Savoy in March the following year to very mixed reviews. It suffered greatly in comparison with their earlier production *The Mikado* which, after a very successful revival at the same theatre, had closed three days earlier. Everyone knew then that it was to be their last joint production. Although some thought it magnificent ('It may claim to stand in the front row of Comic Operas') others thought differently. One critic summed it up, and in doing so summed up their careers: 'The last curtain had fallen on the greatest collaboration in the history of the modern stage'.

–

The Grand Duke closed after 123 performance; it has not been performed on the London stage since. Gilbert and Sullivan's partnership is still unsurpassed, their legacy of operettas very much revered. Sullivan died in 1900, Gilbert in 1911.

96 The LAST of the treadwheel

1898

The Victorian penal system was an area of thoughtful experimentation in which genuine attempts to reform convicts were combined with some extraordinarily futile corrective measures. One of the weirder machines found in most prisons, used for the infliction of hard labour on prisoners, was the treadwheel. Its use was abolished in 1898.

Work in a Victorian prison was monotonous and hard; in some cases it was originally intended to be corrective. It was however usually of the most fruitless kind. If picking oakum, unraveling bits of old rope for use as a caulking material, was the convict's most useful activity, his most useless must surely have been the time he spent on the treadwheel.

The treadwheel was a large iron frame like an elongated water-wheel, around the circumference of which were placed steps. A gang of prisoners was then required to walk the steps, turning the wheel in pointless motion for hours at a time.

A wooden cross-piece onto which the prisoners held kept the gang in unison and each prisoner was set a certain calculated theoretical 'height' to climb in a period of about six hours each day. 10,000 feet was a normal average expectation.

The very young and the very old were excused this exercise but the most disheartening aspect was its futility.

The treadwheel was invented by Mr (later Sir William) Cubitt of Ipswich at the request of the Brixton Prison Governor in 1817 who despaired of finding some hard labour for his convicts.

At one stage many prison authorities, in anticipation of a more modern, 'cost-effective' age, actually tried to sell the power generated by their prisoners by offering the rotating axle projecting from their prison walls to entrepreneurs. The most use it was ever put to though, and only in very few prisons, was to grind some wheat for prison consumption or to pump water to storage tanks.

In the 1870s more and more wheels were built, but their acceptability was soon to fade.

The Gladstone Commission on Prison Reform reported in 1895 and among its many recommendations was the abolition of the treadwheel regime. In Scotland the prison governors had already banished the dreaded machine. The use of treadwheels as routine hard labour was finally stopped in 1898.

They existed in many prisons for some years, monuments to a society which was often long on inventiveness and ingenuity but short on humanity and common-sense.

97 The LAST cavalry charge
2 September 1898

In January 1885 General Gordon, in one of the most celebrated of British defeats, died in Khartoum at the hands of the Mahdi's Dervishes. Two days later a British relief force arrived and the British were evacuated from the Sudan. The Mahdi died soon afterwards and was buried at Omdurman. Khalifa Abdullahi replaced him as the leader of the fanatical Muslim army.

In 1898 Kitchener, with a mixed Egyptian and British army, reconquered the Sudan and exacted revenge for Gordon's death. Near Omdurman, on 1 September, as night fell, Kitchener's army faced the Dervish encampment. On the following day the 21st Lancers were to experience enemy fire for the first time and participate in the last full scale British regimental cavalry charge.

Early the next morning the Dervishes attacked. They were temporarily repulsed and the 21st Lancers, commanded by Lieutenant Colonel Martin, was ordered to move out and prevent any scattered groups of the enemy reaching Omdurman.

The regiment moved off into the desert and immediately encountered a small group of the enemy. Martin gave the command and the 21st Lancers 'wheeled right into line' in a long line abreast – the classic cavalry formation. As they galloped towards the enemy they soon realised that they were heading for a trap. In front of them was a gully filled with 2,000 enemy soldiers, in ranks up to twenty deep, who rose to engage them. It was too late to give any other orders and Martin, at the head of his 320 horsemen, thundered into the unflinching enemy. The fighting soon deteriorated into individual contests, the swords and pistols of the cavalrymen against the muskets and spears of the Dervishes.

The hand-to-hand fighting was exceptionally vicious – when the regiment re-formed, one officer and twenty men lay dead; dozens more were wounded. The young Winston Churchill, future Prime Minister, was one of the troop leaders in the *mêlée*, on attachment from the 4th Hussars. He was one of the very lucky few who escaped without a scratch. Three Victoria Crosses were awarded to members of the regiment for their bravery in the two minutes for which the fight lasted.

The 21st Lancers moved off, dismounted and with their carbines drove off the Dervishes from their position. Later that day Khalifa's dervishes were decisively defeated and by nightfall Kitchener had occupied Omdurman with his troops.

–

Never again was the British cavalry in full regimental strength to indulge in the glory of a galloping charge against the enemy. In the Boer war, the guerrilla tactics of the enemy prevented any large scale manoeuvres of that sort. The machine guns and trenches of the first World War, sixteen years later, showed how ineffective cavalry had become as a massed body. The 21st Lancers later amalgamated with the 7th and are today one of the British Army's armoured regiments.

98 The LAST main line railway

March 1899

Throughout the 19th century Britain there was an explosion in the development of transport. First amongst the methods available to the Victorian traveller was the railway, from its earliest beginnings in the 1820s to the full blooded, fully accepted, nationwide network at the end of the century. The last trunk line in the country to be completed was the Great Central Railway Company's link from the Nottinghamshire coalfields to join with the Metropolitan's link from London at Aylesbury. Marylebone Station, the Railway's new terminus in London, was the last main line station to be constructed in the capital.

The Manchester, Sheffield and Lincolnshire railway, the MS&L,

covered the greater proportion of central England from Southport and Liverpool in the west to Grimsby in the east and Rugby in the south. It had been formed from an amalgamation of several smaller companies in 1846.

The success and expansion of railways at that time were all about alliances. It was to an alliance that the chairman of the MS&L, Sir Edward Watkin, turned to fulfil his grand desire of a 'Manchester to Paris' railway. The vital missing link was, of course, London. He became a member of the board of the Metropolitan Railway and, using his influence, gained access to the capital over the Metropolitan's line between Quainton Road just north of Aylesbury and Harrow-on-the-Hill north of London.

The MS&L built new track from the north to Quainton Road and from Harrow-on-the-Hill to the brand new terminus at Marylebone in north London. On completion of the new link the company was renamed the Great Central Railway.

Marylebone Station, modest by the standards of the other main line stations in London, was opened with great ceremony on 9 March 1899. It had four platforms. The inaugural passenger service from Manchester to Marylebone took place on 15 March.

The Great Central Railway was never a great success in comparison with the larger railway companies but it set standards that were followed. Its rolling stock was considered amongst the best; its slogan 'Rapid Travel in Luxury' began to mean something in the early part of the 20th century. Perhaps the Great Central's greatest achievement was the creation and development of the port of Immingham near Grimsby between 1906 and 1912.

–

The Great Central Railway was absorbed by the London and North Eastern Railway, the LNER in 1923 and nationalised along with all the others in 1948. Marylebone Station then came under the control, in succession, of Eastern Region, Western Region and London Midland Region. It now serves only two suburban lines, to Aylesbury and High Wycombe, but with great gentility. Its listed building frontage and its largely unaltered interior are in great demand by film company's for those tearful departures required in so many of today's 'period' films.

99 The LAST day of the century

31 December 1900

The end of the 19th century came at last – on Monday 31 December 1900. A year earlier, a vigorous correspondence in the columns of *The Times* newspaper and elsewhere had generally come down in favour of the complete year 1900 being the last year of the 19th century and the year 1901 being the first year of the 20th century – a debate, no doubt, to be repeated a hundred years later.

Throughout 1900 Britain was officially preoccupied with the Boer War in South Africa. Celebrations and jollity would undoubtedly have been more widespread without this gloomy millstone around the country's neck. Nevertheless, on the evening of 31 December crowds gathered all over the country in larger numbers than usual. The intention was, of course, to celebrate the passing of the year as well as of the century and to herald the dawning of what was universally hoped to be a new golden age for Britain and her Empire.

In London the main crowd of several thousand assembled outside St Paul's Cathedral. A strong force of police was standing by to prevent too much rowdyism but in the end was not really needed. As the first chimes of 12 o'clock were struck the Scots in the crowd struck up with the usual 'Auld Lang Syne'. This was soon drowned by the roars of the crowd and several other more 'English' songs such as 'The Absent Minded Beggar' and 'They all love Jack'. After the national anthem was sung, the crowd dispersed and moved off towards Ludgate Hill, Fleet Street and the Strand.

–

The Times' leader writer must have passed the last moments of the 19th century dreaming up some flowery language for the occasion: 'The twentieth century has dawned upon us; and as we float past this great landmark on the shores of time, feelings of awe and wonder naturally creep over us. An irresistible impulse impels all but the most frivolous to look before and after as we enter on the stage in the immeasurable process of the suns which begins today.'

100 The LAST Victorian day
– a postscript
22 *January 1901*

The last days of Queen Victoria, were more than the quiet passage from this world of a much-loved and respected monarch. So great was her influence in Britain, the British Empire, in Europe and the world, that her death in the first bleak days of the new century signalled not only the end of a reign but the end of an era.

The Queen spent the Christmas of 1900 at Osborne on the Isle of Wight and saw out the old year there. She was frail and had problems with her eyesight, having to employ one of her granddaughters to make the entries in her famous journal which she had kept for nearly seventy years. A few visitors arrived to see her in January, notably Lord Roberts, home from the Boer War. On 19 January she started to fade and the family were informed. She died peacefully on 22 January, quietly relinquishing the 'splendid burden of Empire which she had borne for so long, and the wearisome shackles of mortality'.

–

Queen Victoria ruled over the largest empire ever known, she reigned for nearly sixty-four years, longer than any other British sovereign. She was just eighteen when her uncle, William IV, died and she began her auspicious and sensible reign. She was eighty-one when she died and the world was a very different place to the one that Princess Alexandrina Victoria, daughter of the Duke of Kent, had known as a child at Kensington Palace, near the beginning of the century. Her own involvement in the changes that had taken place was considerable; she was probably the last sovereign to have had such an influence on the shape of any western nation.

Notice of Queen Victoria's death is attached to the railings outside Buckingham Palace. Stunned Londoners, pressing close to read it for themselves, realised even then that they were witnessing the end of a unique period.

Select bibliography

Allen, J *Battles of the British Navy, Vol II* Bohn 1852

Archibald, E H H *The Fighting Ship in the Royal Navy 897-1984* Blandford Press

Aronson, T *Grandmama of Europe* Cassell 1973

Aspinall, A (Ed) *English Historical Documents, Vol XI, 1783-1832* Eyre & Spottiswoode 1959

Baines, Anthony (Ed) *Musical Instruments Through the Ages* Pelican 1978

Baldick, Robert *The Duel* Spring Books 1965

Barnes, R M *A History of the Regiments and Uniforms of the British Army* Seeley Service & Co

Beales, D *From Castlereagh to Gladstone 1815-1885* Nelson 1969

Bellew, G *Britain's Kings and Queens* Piktin Pictorials 1971

Benson, E F *Queen Victoria* Longmans Green & Co 1935

Bonavia, Michael R *Historic Railway Sites in Britain* Robert Hale 1987

Bond, B (Ed) *Victorian Military Campaigns* Hutchinson 1967

Bradbury, F *Guide to British and Irish Silver Marks* J W Northend 1973

Brahms, C *Gilbert and Sullivan* Weidenfeld & Nicholson 1975

Brogan, H *History of the United States of America* Longman 1985

Brooke-Little, J *Royal Ceremonies of State* Country Life Books 1980

Butler, Audrey *Everyman's Dictionary of Dates* J M Dent & Son 1984

Campbell, Bruce *The Oxford Book of Birds* OUP 1964

Clark, T D *Frontier America* Charles Scribner's Sons 1959

Clowes, W Laird *The Royal Navy, a History, Vols IV & V* Sampson Low, Marston & Co 1899

Colledge, J J *Ships of The Royal Navy, Vol I* David & Charles 1969

Cook, C & Stevenson, J *The Longmans Handbook of Modern British History 1714-1980* Longmans 1983

Cowie, L W *A Dictionary of British Social History* G Bell & Sons 1973

Critchley, T A *A History of Police in England and Wales* Constable 1967

Cunnington, C & P & Beard, C *A Dictionary of English Costume, 900-1900* Adam & Charles Black 1960

Essberger, S *Monopoly London* Chameleon Publishing 1987

Ewing, Elizabeth *Everyday Dress, 1650-1900* Batsford 1984

Fido, Martin *The Crimes, Detection and Death of Jack the Ripper* Weidenfeld & Nicholson 1987

Fisher, James (Ed) *Thorburn's Birds* Mermaid Books 1982

Fleischer, N & Andre, S *A Pictorial History of Boxing* Hamlyn 1987

Flower, R & Wynne Jones, M *One Hundred Years of Motoring* RAC 1981

Gardner, Brian *The East India Company* Rupert Hart-Davis 1971

Godwin, Peter *Sailing Man-of-War 1650-1850* Conway Maritime 1987

Gregg, Pauline *A Social and Economic History of Britain 1760-1972* Harrap 1950-73

Hague, D B & Christie, R *Lighthouses, their Architecture, History & Archeology* Gomer Press 1975

Heap, C & Van Riemsdijk, J *The Pre-Grouping Railways, Pt 2* HMSO 1980

Hibbert, C *Highwaymen* Weidenfeld & Nicholson

Hibbert, C *Tower of London* Readers Digest Association 1971
Hibbs, John *The History of British Bus Services* David & Charles 1968
Holmes, T W *The Semaphore* Arthur H Stockwell Ltd 1983
Huggett, F E *A Dictionary of British History, 1815-1973* Basil Blackwell 1974
Hughes, R *The Fatal Shore* Pan (Collins) 1987
Jackson, Derick *Lighthouses of England and Wales* David & Charles 1975
Lloyd, Christopher *The British Seaman* Collins 1968
Louda, J & Maclagan, M *Lines of Succession* Orbis Publishing 1981
MacKenzie, N & J *Dickens, A Life* Oxford Universtity Press 1979
Mahan, A T *The Life of Nelson* Sampson, Low & Co 1897
Marcombe, David *The Victorian Sailor* Shire Publications 1985
Massie, A *Byron's Travels* Sidwick & Jackson 1988
Milton, R *The English Ceremonial Book* David & Charles 1972
Montague-Smith, Patrick (Ed) *Debrett's Peerage & Baronetage* Debrett's Peerage 1979
Montague-Smith, Patrick *The Royal Line of Succession* Piktin Pictorials 1970
Morrison, I *Boxing, the Records* Guiness Books 1986
Newark, P *Sabre & Lance* Blandford Press 1987
Priestley, Philip *Victorian Prison Lives* Methuen 1985
Purvey, P F (Ed) *Coins of England and the United Kingdom* Seaby 1984
Quennell, M & C H B *A History of Everyday Things in England, Vols III & IV* Batsford 1934
Reilly, Robin *Pitt the Younger* Cassell 1978
Royston Pike, E *Britain's Prime Ministers from Walpole to Wilson* Odhams 1968
Rumbelow, Donald *I Spy Blue* Cedric Chivers 1971
Sadie, Stanley (Ed) *The New Grove Dictionary of Musical Instruments* MacMillan Press Limited 1984
Schick, I T (Ed) *Battledress* Weidenfeld & Nicholson 1978
Soar, Phil *Encyclopedia of British Football* Willow Books 1987
Sutcliffe, S *Martello Towers* David & Charles 1972
Tomlin, E W F *Charles Dickens 1812-1870* Weidenfeld & Nicholson 1969
Trevelyan, G M *English Social History* Longmans Green & Co 1946
Trevelyan, G M *History of England* Longmans Green & Co 1926
Trotter, William Pym *The Royal Navy in Old Photographs* J M Dent & Sons 1975
Tyler, Martin *The Story of Football* Marshall Cavendish 1976
Vincent, B *Haydn's Dictionary of Dates* Ward, Lock & Co 1910
Walford, Edward *Old and New London, Vol VI* Cassell Petter & Galpin 1870
Weinreb, B & Hibbert, C (Ed) *The London Encyclopedia* MacMillan 1983
Williams, Neville *Chronology of the Modern World, 1763 to the present time* Barrie & Rockliff 1966
Woodcock, T & Robinson, J M *The Oxford Guide to Heraldry* Oxford University Press 1988
Wragg, David W *Flight before Flying* Osprey 1974
Ziegler, Philip *King William IV* Collins 1971
Cassell's Illustrated History of England, Vols VI to IX Cassell Petter & Galpin 1873
The Comprehensive History of England, Vol IV Blackie & Son 1861
The Encyclopedia Brittanica
Folklore, Myths and Legends of Britain Readers Digest Association 1973
Heritage of Britain Readers Digest Association 1975

Index

Figures in **bold** indicate illustrations.

Index

173

Index